DAMMIT!

Play GUITAR DAMMIT!

Matt Scharfglass

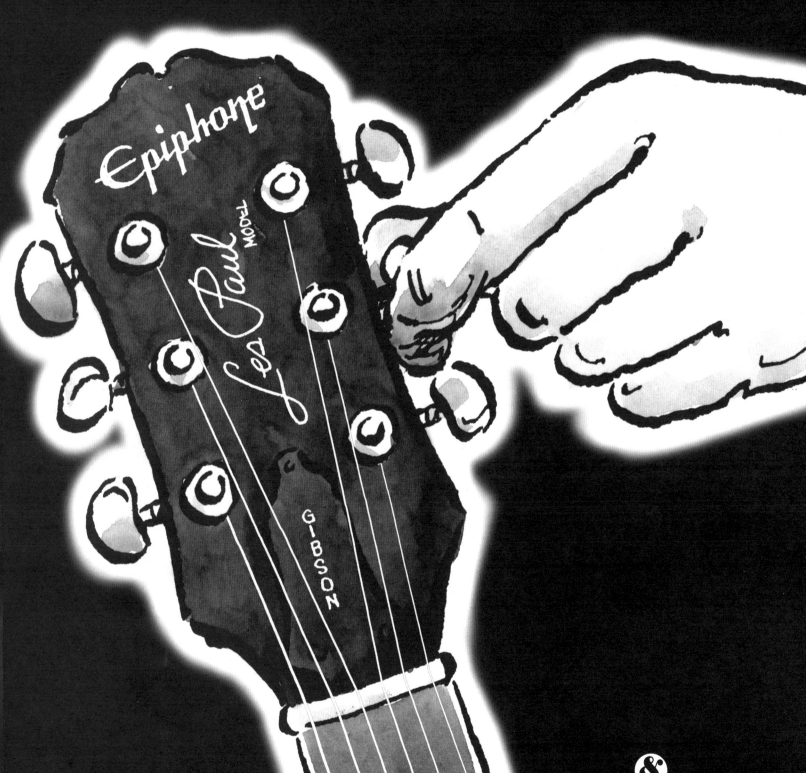

WISE PUBLICATIONS
part of The Music Sales Group

London / New York /
Paris / Sydney / Copenhagen / Berlin /
Madrid / Tokyo

Published by
WISE PUBLICATIONS
8/9 Frith Street,
London W1D 3JB, England.

Exclusive Distributors:

Music Sales Limited
Distribution Centre,
Newmarket Road, Bury St Edmunds,
Suffolk IP33 3YB, England.

Music Sales Corporation
257 Park Avenue South,
New York, NY10010,
United States of America.

Music Sales Pty Limited
120 Rothschild Avenue,
Rosebery, NSW 2018, Australia.

Order No. AM975359
ISBN 0-7119-9661-X
This book © Copyright 2004 by
Wise Publications.
Music © Copyright 2004
Dorsey Brothers Music Limited.
All Rights Reserved.
International Copyright Secured.

Written by Matt Scharfglass.
Edited by Tom Fleming.
Designed by Michael Bell Design.
Music processed by Paul Ewers Music Design.
Illustrations by Andy Hammond.
Photography by George Taylor.
Modelled by Jonas Persson & Tom Fleming.
Epiphone Les Paul guitar courtesy of
Scott Avery at Music Ground Limited.
Printed in Malta by Interprint Limited.

Your Guarantee of Quality:
As publishers, we strive to produce every
book to the highest commercial standards.
The music has been freshly engraved
and the book has been carefully designed
to minimise awkward page turns and to
make playing from it a real pleasure.
Particular care has been given to specifying
acid-free, neutral-sized paper made
from pulps which have not been elemental
chlorine bleached. This pulp is from farmed
sustainable forests and was produced with
special regard for the environment.
Throughout, the printing and binding have
been planned to ensure a sturdy, attractive
publication which should give years of
enjoyment. If your copy fails to meet our
high standards, please inform us and we will
gladly replace it.

www.musicsales.com

ABOUT THE AUTHOR

Matt Scharfglass is a New York-based songwriter, bassist, guitarist and multi-instrumentalist. In addition to leading his band, Mrs. Grundy, he keeps himself busy by doing session work and performing all around the New York City area playing anything from show tunes in the shiny Theatre District to loud rock in the grungy East Village.

In 1993 Matt began transcribing and arranging guitar and bass music; hundreds of his transcriptions have appeared worldwide in *Guitar World* magazine and in books published by Warner Brothers, Hal Leonard, Music Sales and Cherry Lane. He is currently the associate music editor at *Guitar World* and a senior editor at *Guitar World Acoustic*.

Matt's other books include *Beginning Blues Bass*, *First Step: Guitar For Kids*, *How to Tune Your Guitar* and *The Gig Bag Book of Practical Pentatonics*.

Mrs. Grundy's latest record, *Don't Pick It Up*, was released in 2003. Follow Matt and the band's exploits at www.mrsgrundy.com.

Thanks...
This book could never have happened without:
The support and encouragement of Ed Lozano, Peter Pickow and Dan Earley at Music Sales.
The understanding of Jimmy Brown at *Guitar World*.
The love and patience of my beautiful wife, Sandra Dubrov.

CD Acknowledgements
Narration by Paul Vassallo.
All music composed and performed by Matt Scharfglass.

MUSICAL EXAMPLES

CD TRACK LIST

CD 1

DAMMIT!

USING THIS BOOK

I was walking to the subway after a gig one evening when a scraggly-looking guy carrying a cheap electric guitar (without a case) approached me. Seeing that I was carrying an instrument myself, the man was eager to strike up a conversation. No more than two sentences into it, however, he began to lecture me on the importance of knowing every possible scale and mode. Having lived in New York and its environs my whole life, I've learned how to maintain a "do not engage" stance when dealing with know-it-all (and apparently intoxicated) strangers on the street; I smiled and nodded politely, thinking I would soon be on my train and away from this fellow's incessant chattering. It had been a long day and I was tired; when I realised after about five minutes that he wasn't really on his way to anywhere in particular, the thought of having him follow me any further took over. I interrupted him.

"Ever heard of a guy named Bob Dylan?" I asked. He looked at me blankly. "When was the last time you heard him play a scale? In his entire career he's used probably four, maybe five basic chords, tops." With that, I left him standing on the sidewalk, confused. With this experience in mind, I designed this book to include hundreds of scales and modal exercises - HA! – just kidding! Moving on…

You've tinkered with the guitar; perhaps you became quite good at it, but it got pushed to the side over the years. Or maybe you simply didn't get very far with it and became frustrated and uninterested. Either way, the fact that you're reading this shows that you'd like to get back into it, so this book is for you. Whether you're just returning to the guitar after several years, or you've been playing for a little while and you just want to get better, my goal is to have you spinning off chords, riffs, even solos, in as little time (and with as little hair loss) as possible. While this book assumes you have some basic musical knowledge, don't sweat the reading part of it too much as a CD is included so you can hear the musical examples and play along. You can also freely skip around from section to section to suit your own pace. This book is to be played, not studied; you will not be bogged down with theory.

My only suggestion before beginning is to have your guitar examined and set up for maximum playability by a professional guitar technician. I've seen many guitar and bass students give up quickly under the misconception that they have no musical ability whatsoever, when in reality the instruments they were playing were simply in crappy condition. The expense (which actually isn't too bad) is quite worth it.

That said, I hope you enjoy the music offered in this book. I think the best way to learn to play is to, well, play, so let's get to it.

TECHNIQUE BASICS

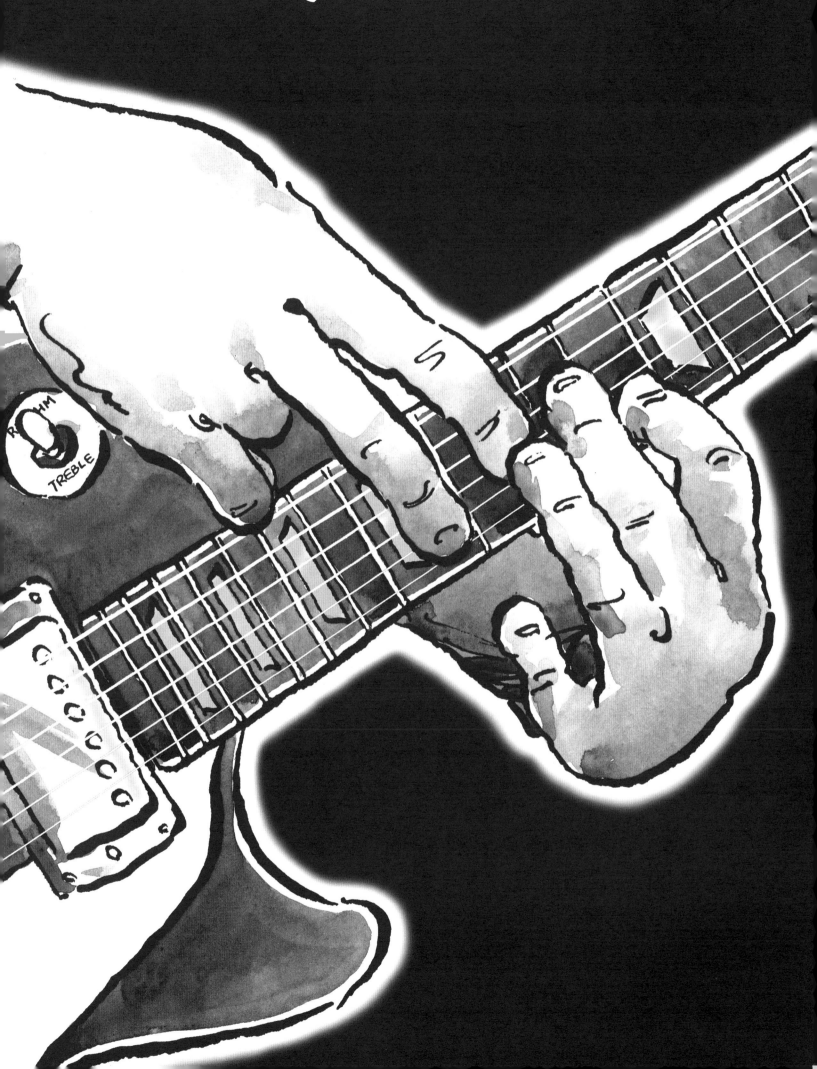

TECHNIQUE BASICS

RELAX...

In spite of everything you
may have been told by guitar
teachers about correct
posture, hand position etc,
there are actually as many
ways to hold and play the
guitar as there are guitarists:
sitting down, standing up,
lying down...

...the most important
thing is that you should feel
comfortable. Relax.

I SAID RELAX, DAMMIT!

LEFT HAND

Classical technique stresses that the thumb of your left hand should stay 'anchored' to the middle of the neck.

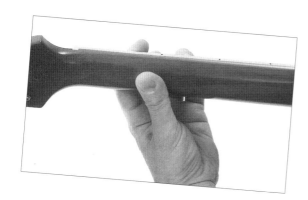

Rock and jazz guitarists, however, frequently bring the thumb way up over the top of the neck, for extra strength when bending notes, to mute the bottom string, and even to supply the bottom note of an otherwise tricky chord. You'll find examples of 'thumb' chords later in this book.

Letting your thumb stray below the centre line, however, is generally not a good idea. It just doesn't give you the strength you need.

RIGHT HAND

Most rock players use a pick (plectrum) at least most of the time. These come in various sizes and thicknesses, even in unusual materials such as metal and stone.

Get hold of a selection of them and fiddle around to see what works for you. Many people find that thinner gauges work best for relaxed strumming and thicker gauges give more attack for precise picking.

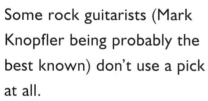

Some rock guitarists (Mark Knopfler being probably the best known) don't use a pick at all.

Others use the plectrum between the thumb and first finger while picking with the remaining fingers.

Wes Montgomery played everything with only his thumb, spreading his fingers out for support.

For some picking styles you may want to rest your hand near the bridge so that all the movement is in your hand. For strummy stuff you'll probably want to use your whole arm.

So it's really up to you. Don't worry about it too much. If it feels comfortable, it's probably fine.

Pull up a chair, grab your preferred liquid refreshment, put the cat out, sit back and play guitar... **DAMMIT!**

DAMMIT!

TYPES OF GUITAR

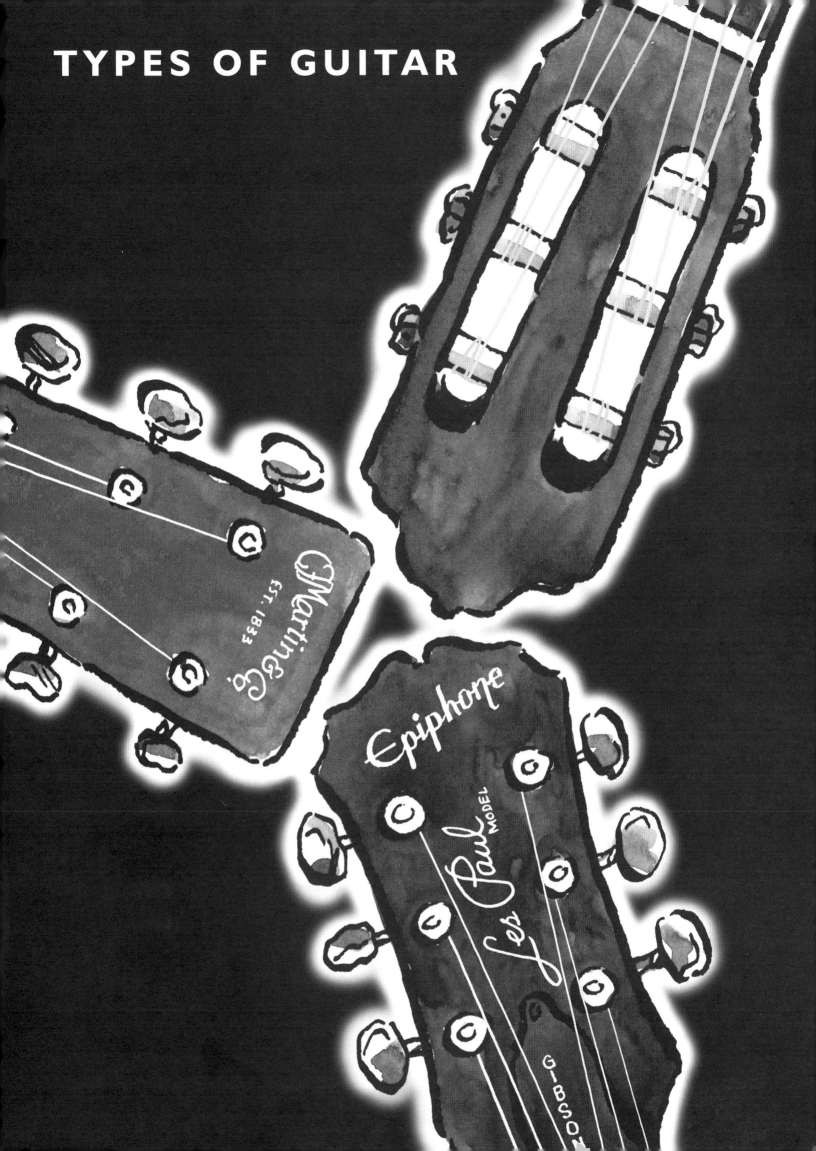

TYPES OF GUITAR

Chances are you already know what type of guitar you have and the other types that are out there; feel free to skip ahead. However, you may find this information useful for perhaps making a decision on a new purchase or simply for curiosity's sake.

STEEL-STRING ACOUSTIC

Favoured by countless folk-influenced players (Bob Dylan, Joni Mitchell, Stephen Stills, Ani DiFranco... you get the picture). Also used by jazz artists (Al DiMeola and John McLaughlin). Rockers have made their mark with it as well (Jimmy Page, Dave Matthews and all points in between). Perfect campfire instrument; has a bright, metallic tone.

NYLON-STRING ACOUSTIC

Heard predominantly in flamenco music (Paco DeLucia), classical (pick any classical guitarist) and world music (Gipsy Kings). Played pretty much exclusively without a pick (fingers only). Has a mellow, darker, softer tone than its steel-string counterpart. *Très* sophisticated.

ELECTRIC

Ah, yes. The scourge of parents and schoolteachers everywhere. There are so many different kinds that a brief background is in order. Generally, for most guitarists, there are only two brands: Fender and Gibson. Of course, this is ridiculous, as many worthy guitar manufacturers such as Ibanez, Gretsch, Hamer, ESP, Paul Reed Smith and Rickenbacker (among countless others I've neglected) have contributed substantially to modern music history and continue to be strong fixtures in the guitar market.

However, the electric guitar originated with Fender and Gibson, and consequently most other electric guitars are simply considered variations on their themes.

As you've probably guessed, Fenders and Gibsons can be prohibitively expensive. With Fender boasting a user list with the likes of Eric Clapton, Jimi Hendrix and Stevie Ray Vaughan and Gibsons appearing in immortal rock photos from the '60s, '70s and '80s with Jimmy Page, Angus Young, Pete Townshend and Slash, the reputations of these two companies certainly aren't undeserved.

Both manufacturers produce fine instruments and if you have the cheese, go for it. However, many other guitar makers, like those mentioned earlier, produce instruments of the same quality (though perhaps without the same colourful histories) for substantially less dough. Especially since the late '90s rise of guitar-oriented heavy rock, the quality and popularity of the lower-priced guitar is at a high.

Okay, history lesson over... **LET'S PLAY!**

EH, NOT SO FAST, JUNIOR

Sorry, but you're going to have to tune up that thing before you turn up that thing. This is purely optional of course, but it's probably a wise move to be in tune with the accompanying CD if you're planning on playing along with it (unless you're deliberately going for that trashy, devil-may-care Johnny Thunders or Neil Young vibe).

I've provided reference pitches on tracks 1-6 of the CD. Since each pitch is on its own track, you can set your CD player to repeat the track if necessary so you'll have as much time as you need to tune the string.

READY TO ROCK?

 LOW E TUNING NOTE

Track 1

 A TUNING NOTE

Track 2

 D TUNING NOTE

Track 3

 G TUNING NOTE

Track 4

 B TUNING NOTE

Track 5

 HIGH E TUNING NOTE

Track 6

CHORDS

CHORDS...
(AND NOT JUST DOOFY CAMPFIRE ONES, EITHER)

Ninety percent of everything you play will be based on chords. Guitar solos, while mighty and fearsome, only last for a relative few seconds (unless you're Joe Satriani or you're playing *'Free Bird'*); besides, you can't accompany a vocal or other melody by yourself without chords. So for the next 20 or so pages, I'll not only show you (or reacquaint you with) the basics, but I'll throw in some stuff that sounds so cool (while remaining so easy to play it's silly) that people will think you've been playing consistently for years. Depending on your skill level, you may wish to skip around; by all means, feel free to do so.

A quick note for your reference: chord shapes are often referred to as *open* or *movable*. Open shapes involve open strings (this section on *Campfire Chords* provides plenty of examples), while movable shapes are exactly that: no open strings, and the same shape can be used anywhere on the fretboard (see the section on *barre chords*, for instance).

CAMPFIRE CHORDS

These are the aforementioned basics. They're appropriate for sing-alongs, sit-ins, road trips and, well, campfires. We'll start with some easy ones. The following musical examples use these six chords in very common settings.

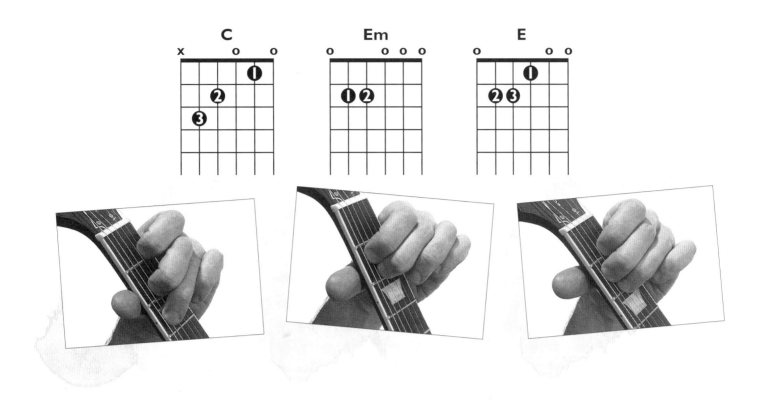

I USED TO LOVE PLAYING GUITAR

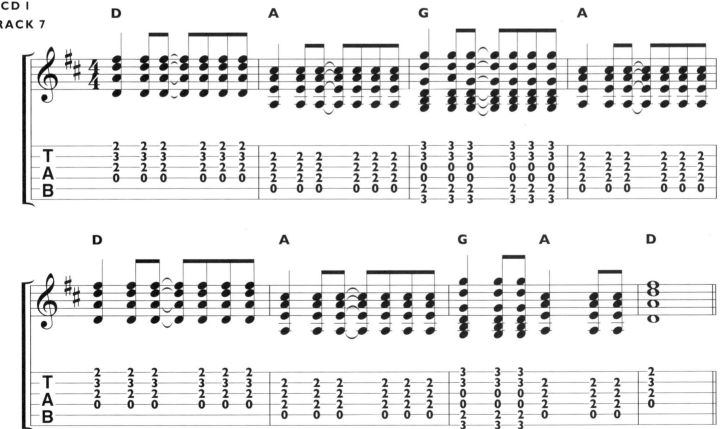

ADRIAN! ADRIAN!

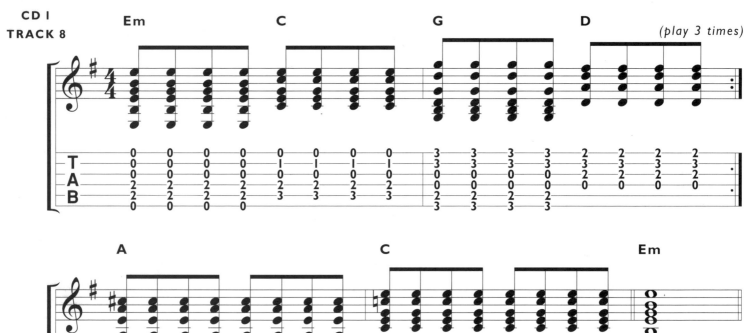

WHAT I LIKE ABOUT LOLA ROCKIN' IN THE USA

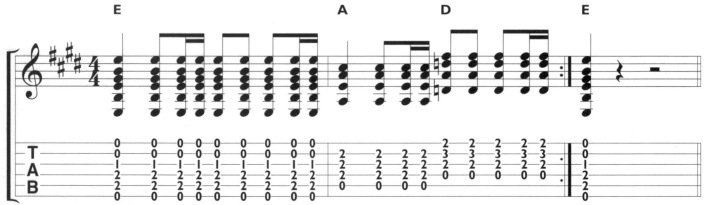

The next example is comprised mostly of minor chords. When shifting from the **D minor** to the **G7**, use your index finger as a *pivot finger* – keeping it stationary will make changing from one chord to the next easier.

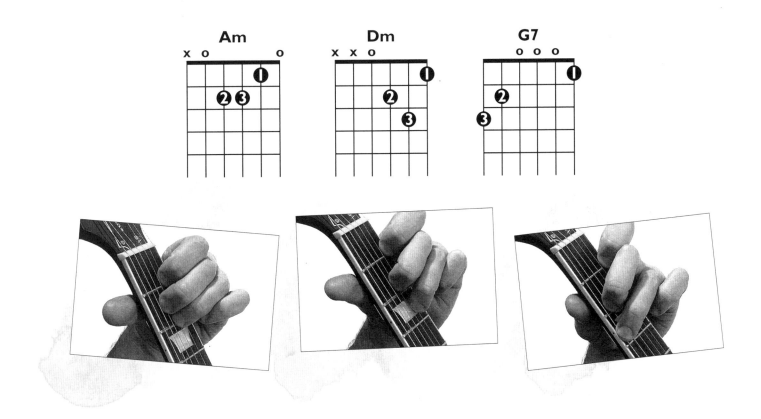

COUNTING JANGLES

CD 1
TRACK 10

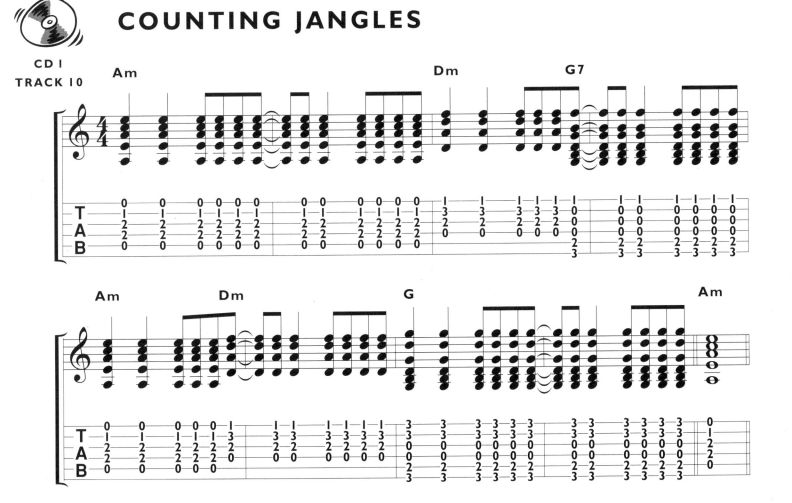

Here's a simple but funky blues groove using another **7th** chord.

C7

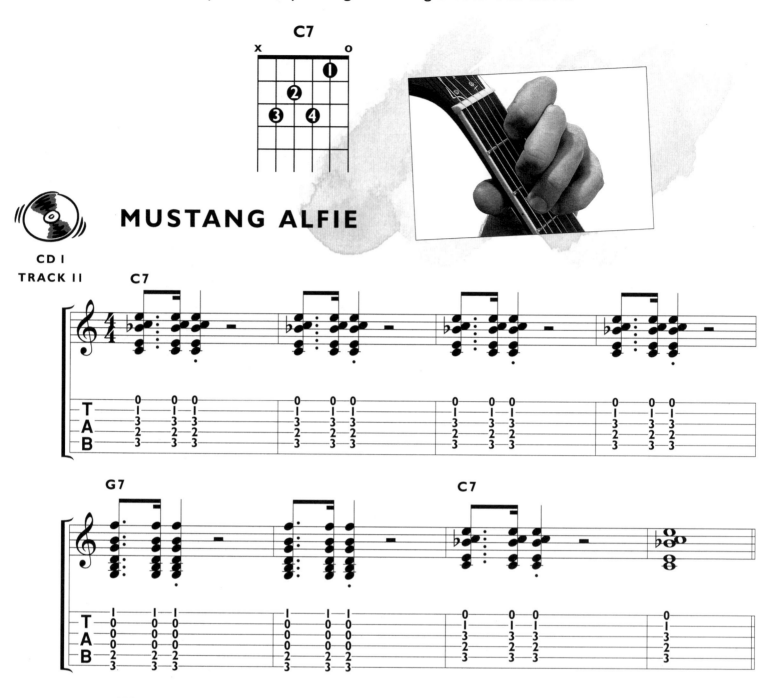

MUSTANG ALFIE

Wanna wrap this up with a little bluegrass? I thought so.

D7   **A7**   **E7**

26

FIDDLE WITH THIS

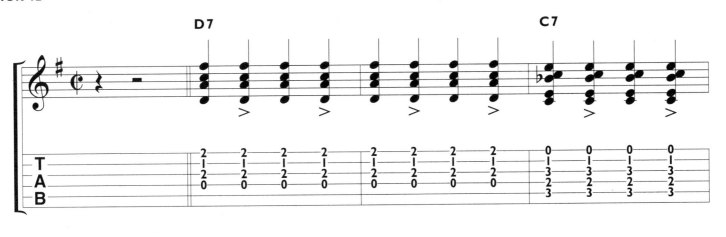

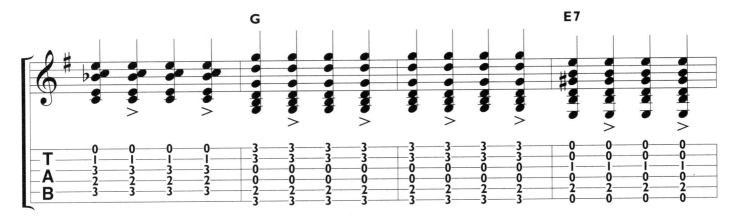

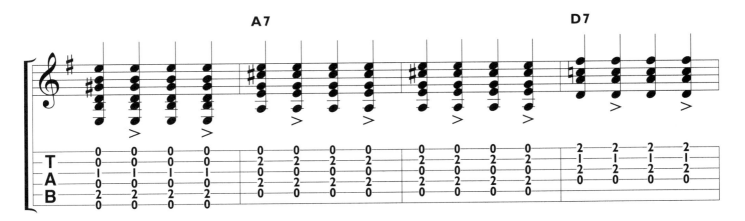

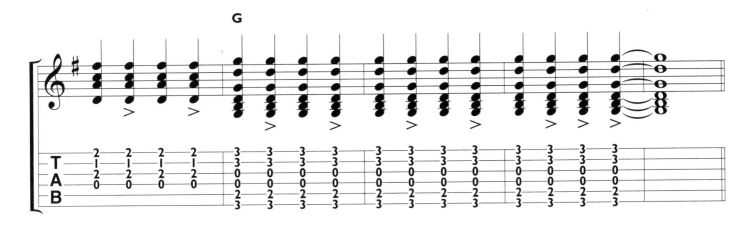

BARRE CHORDS

Yes, it's pronounced "bar"; I don't know why they spell it in that funny way. Anyway, these chord grips are so named because they are played by pressing down on several strings with the same finger; to do this, the finger must be used as a bar of sorts. The 'barre' finger is indicated with a loop in the chord diagrams you will see throughout this section.

This is a major barre chord shape.

The barre chords' selling point: they are movable, so you can shift from one chord to the next without having to rearrange your fingers, as shown in the next musical example.

CD 1
TRACK 13

HE ALWAYS KEPT A FULLY STOCKED BARRE

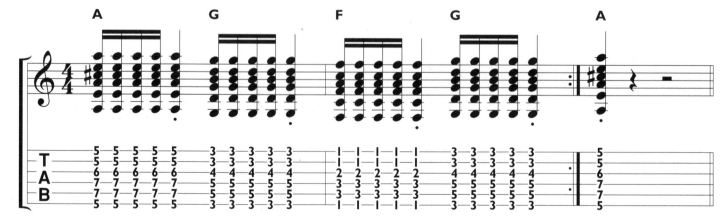

28

Many times, a guitarist will opt to omit the top two notes of a full barre chord for a couple of reasons: (a) in heavy rock, these notes may add too much 'jangle' to the overall sound, and (b) it's simply easier to fret the bottom four notes than it is to barre the entire width of the fretboard. The following shape therefore isn't technically a barre chord, but it does originate from it and thus its inclusion in this section.

By way of example: the popular Lenny Kravitz song *Fly Away* is composed entirely of this 'barre-minus-the-top-two-strings' chord... begin by playing this shape at the 5th fret, then shift up to the 7th fret, then the 8th fret, back down to the 3rd fret, scoot back up to the 10th fret and bam! bang! pwifft! Instant hit.

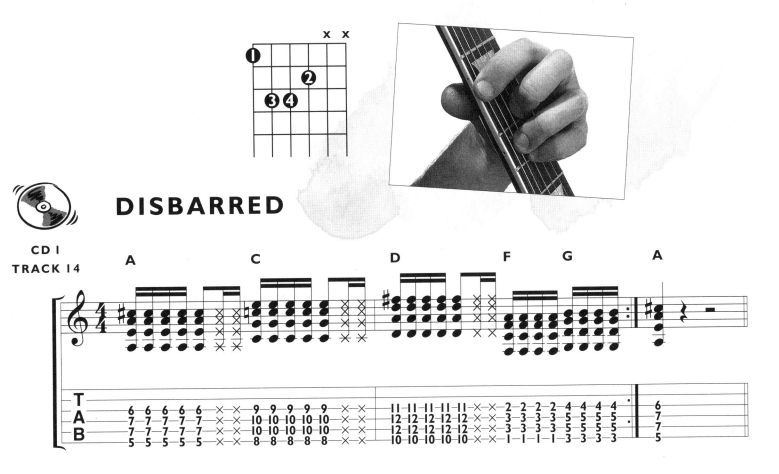

CD 1
TRACK 14

DISBARRED

This type of major barre shape is played on the middle four strings; it is quite popular due to its ease of use. Again, it's movable, so you can play any major chord you want by simply shifting up or down the desired number of frets.

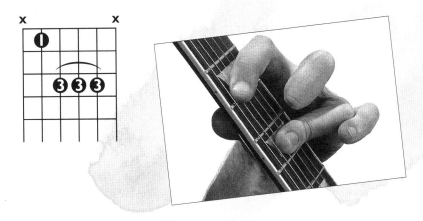

This next mini-song will not only show you a context in which this chord is used, it'll also help you with that Pete Townshend windmill manoeuvre.

WHO BARRE YOU

CD 1
TRACK 15

Barre chords also come in minor flavours. Here are some shapes for a rainy afternoon.

The following makes use of all the barre chord shapes we've covered...

LET'S GO BARRE-HOPPING

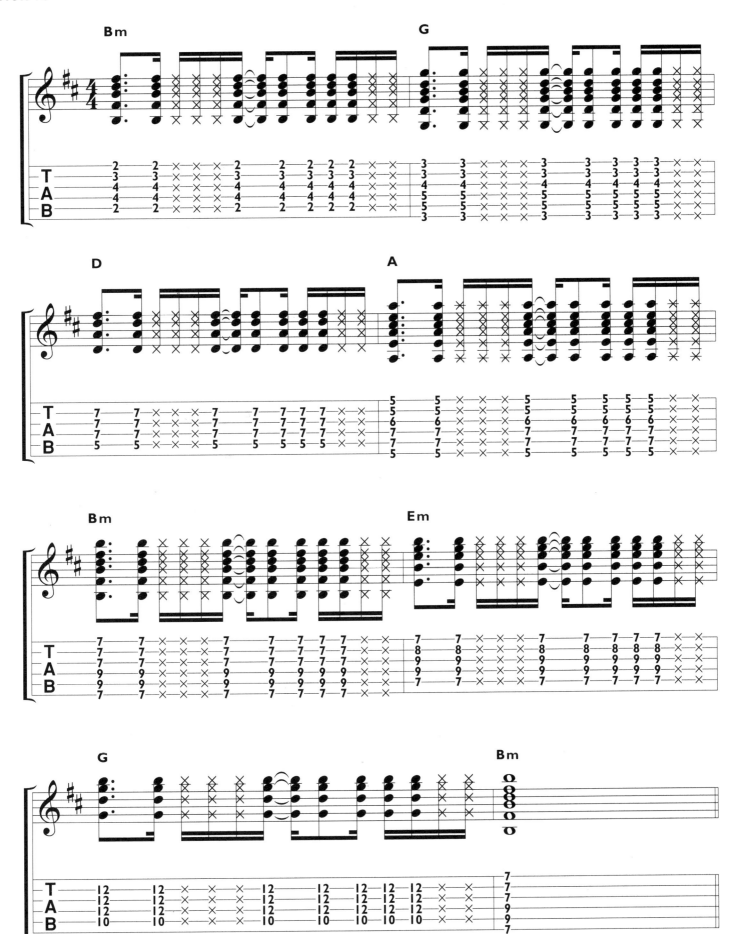

Hey! Let's close out this section with some really fun *point / counterpoint* about barre chords!

BOO

Some people find barre chords harder to play and prefer to stick to 'regular' open chords.

YAY!

Others like the fact that barre grips are movable and therefore enable the player to fret different chords without having to adjust the fingers.

BOO

Due to the open strings, a regular **A minor** *'campfire chord'*, for example, has more shimmer than an **A minor** barre chord played at the 5th fret.

YAY!

On the other hand, it's impossible to play any full **C minor** chord (for instance) without barring.

TOP-VOICED CHORDS

Chords don't necessarily have to be played in their full forms. In fact, mixing it up a bit by playing different versions (known as *voicings*) of the same chord helps to keep a guitar part interesting. Although the chord voicings you will learn in this section are appropriate anywhere outside of your Slayer tribute band, they are used most predominantly in reggae, ska, funk and even disco.

In a nutshell, each one of these chords is played on the three high strings. And they're movable! The following illustrations depict the basic top-voiced major shapes.

Let's start off with an easy, laid-back reggae groove. Use the shape shown in the first chord box above to play each of these chords.

CD I
TRACK 17

STUFFED SPEEDO

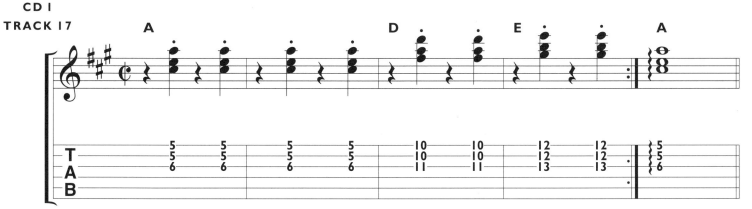

Top-voiced chords can be used very effectively to complement another guitar part in a song. In the next example, check out how the top guitar adds a bit of sonic sparkle to the bottom guitar.

HIDE THE GLITTER, HERE COMES ZIGGY

Pretty easy, right? Well, top-voiced minor chords are just as simple.

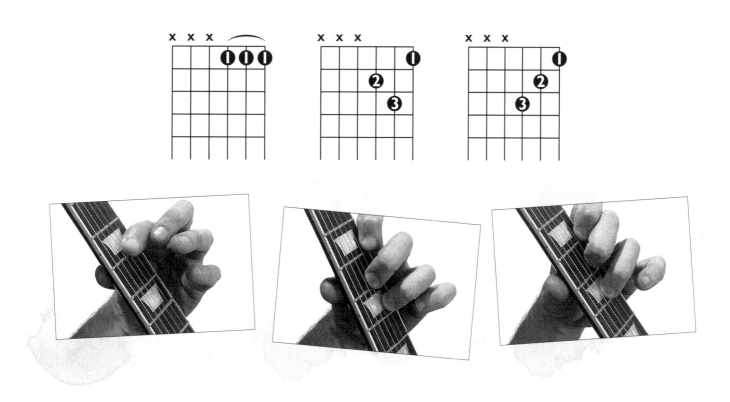

Behold the power and simplicity of these minor shapes!

LAZY SKANKING

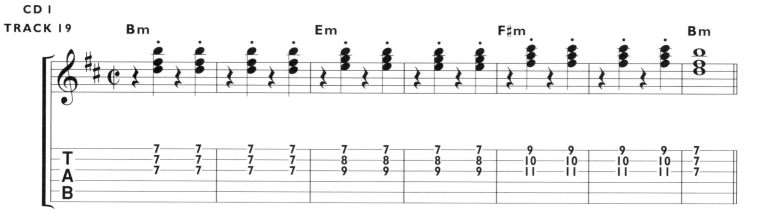

Check out how minor shapes are used to bring the on da funk in what is actually an E *major* groove.

CD 1
TRACK 20

GIVE THE CLARINET PLAYER SOME (BREAK IT DOWN!)

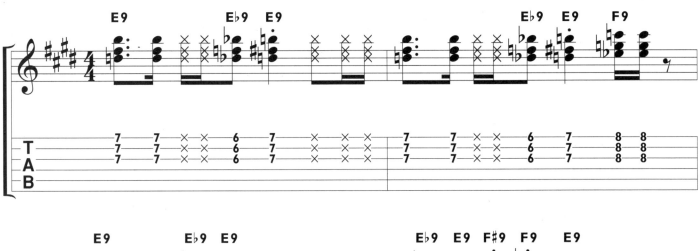

The opposite applies as well… you can create even more textures by playing major shapes over minor chords, as shown in the following.

CD 1
TRACK 21

PUT DOWN THE CHEESE AND STEP AWAY FROM THE BUFFET TABLE

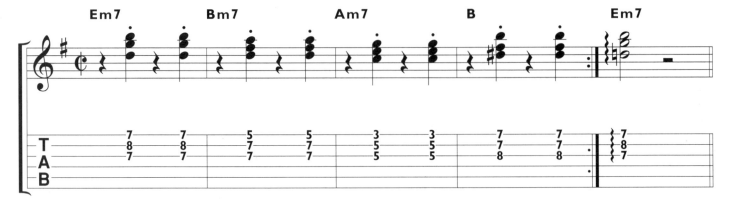

And now, a couple of blasts of old-school rhythm 'n' blues for your listening and playing pleasure.

HEY BABY, WHERE'D YOU PUT MY THANG

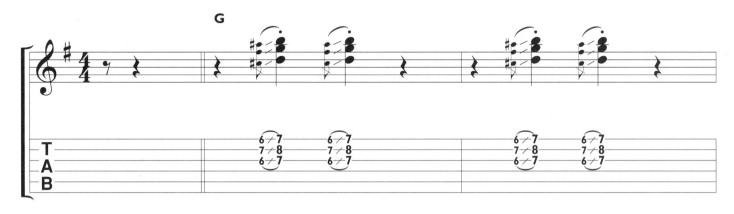

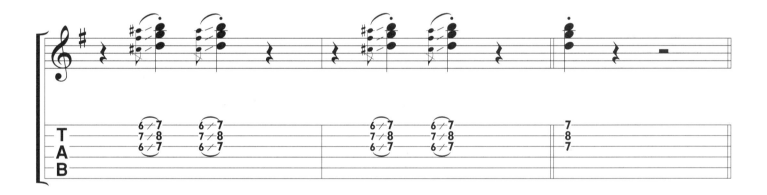

AIN'T NOTHIN' RHYMES WITH 'AMONGST'

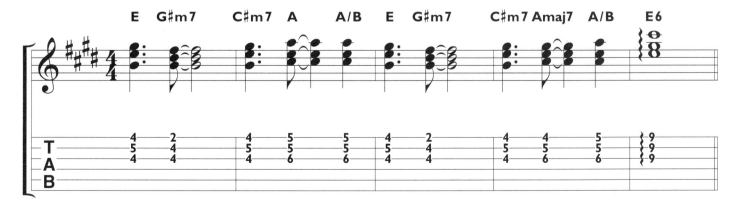

SUSPENDED AND 'ADD' CHORDS

Suspended chords (more commonly referred to as 'sus' chords) are neither major nor minor. They come in two varieties: **sus2** or **sus4**, and usually lead into a major or minor chord.

The **Dsus4**, **Dsus2**, **Esus4** and **A7sus4** chords are among the most widely used sus chords by guitarists. Play through the following mini-song and you'll see why.

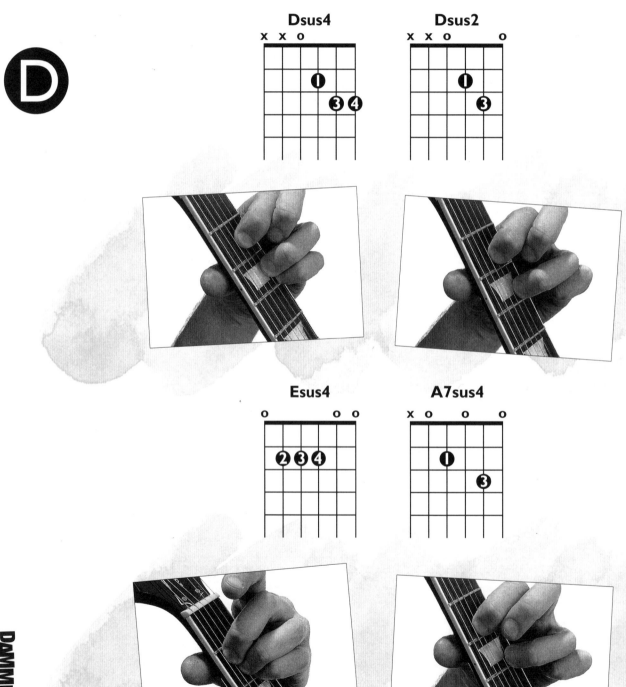

Dsus4

Dsus2

Esus4

A7sus4

SUSPENDED WITHOUT PAY

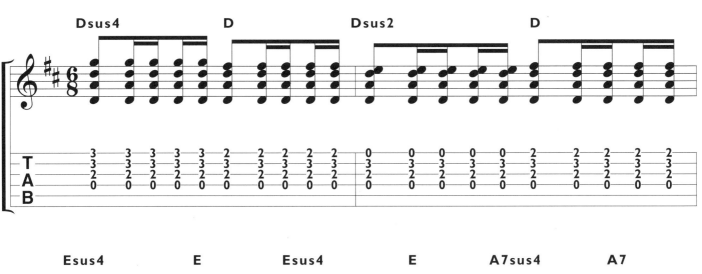

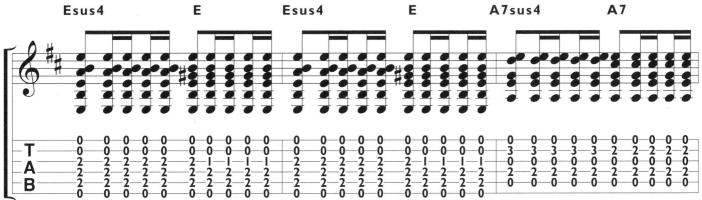

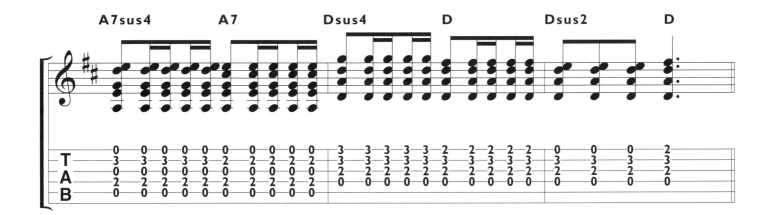

The sus chords in *'Suspended Without Pay'* all lead into major chords; in our next example you'll hear how they work with minor chords. Here are a couple more chords for you.

Asus4

Asus2

A little playing hint: Take a look at the music to the following opus, *'Suspenders of Freedom.'* The transition from the **A minor** chord to the **Esus4** chord (going from the first bar into the second bar) can be done seamlessly by using the middle and ring fingers of the fretting hand as *pivot fingers* (finger positions that are common to two or more chords).

Also, notice how the **Asus2** chord at the end emotes a feeling of, well, um, *suspense.* Is it major or minor? No one really knows…

SUSPENDERS OF FREEDOM

CD 1
TRACK 25

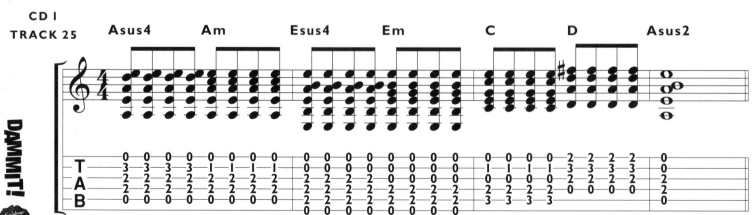

'Add' chords are major or minor chords that contain an extra note; as with sus chords, this note is either the second or the fourth but usually called **add9** or **add11**. (More 'add' chords are covered in the next section, *Dressed-Up Chords*.)

The **Cadd9** and **Csus2** chords are very popular among rock guitarists because they allow for pivot fingerings, especially when played in context with **D** and **G** chords.

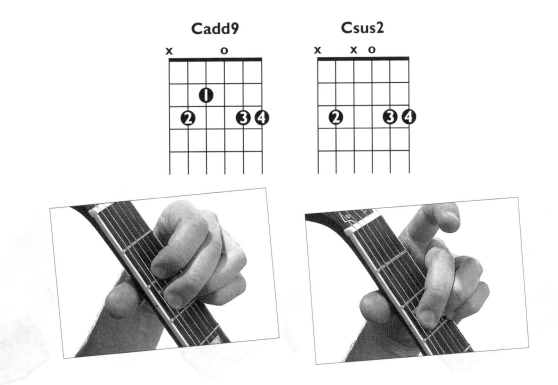

CD 1
TRACK 26

MORE THAN THE FEELING OF YOU SHAKING ME ALL NIGHT LONG

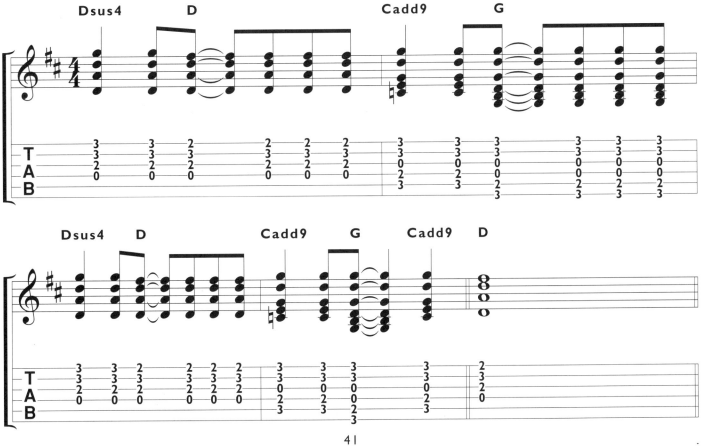

41

Feel like getting fancy? In some cases it's easy to have a sus or 'add' chord containing a both a 2nd and a 4th. The following chord frames illustrate how these are played, along with another **sus2** chord.

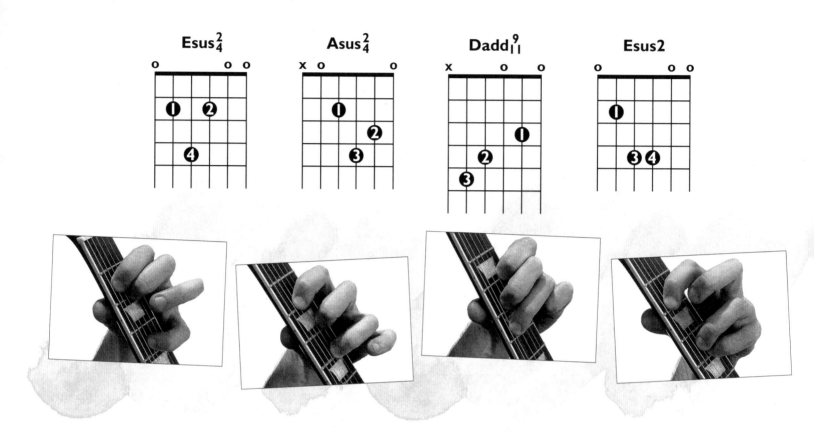

Esus$\frac{2}{4}$ Asus$\frac{2}{4}$ Dadd$^{9}_{11}$ Esus2

THE ADDED SUSPENSE IS KILLING ME

CD I
TRACK 27

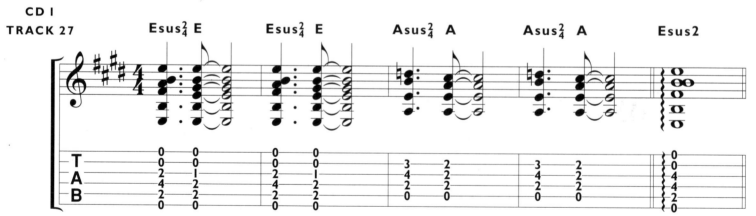

Esus$\frac{2}{4}$ E   Esus$\frac{2}{4}$ E   Asus$\frac{2}{4}$ A   Asus$\frac{2}{4}$ A   Esus2

Since 'Suspenders of Freedom' was such a monumental success, I've decided to reprise it with a new chord in the third measure. Hope you like it.

SUSPENDERS OF FREEDOM AND CAKE

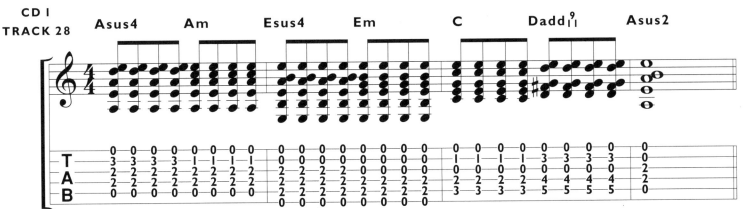

Oops! Almost forgot another cool sus chord. Check out how well it works with that fancy-schmancy $Dadd^9_{11}$ chord.

E7sus4

THANK YOU VERY MUCH, GOOD NIGHT

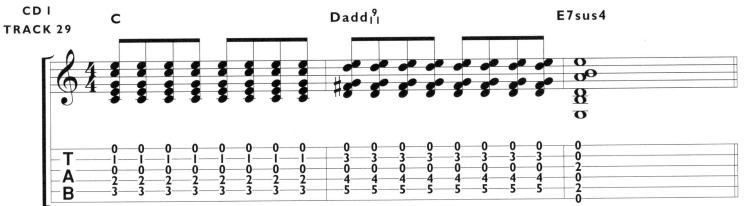

'DRESSED-UP' CHORDS

These are really just ordinary major and minor voicings sprinkled with an extra note or two for added tonal colour.

Besides introducing some new chords, the musical examples in this section utilise many of the types we've covered thus far; refer back to sections **A** and **D** if you need a quick refresher on these chords.

This section also introduces us to chords with weird names such as, for example, **Dm/F**. The English translation of this is **D minor over F**. The English translation of that translation is simply play a **D minor** chord, and add an **F** note to the bottom. Likewise, **Bm(add11)/A** means play a **Bm(add11)** chord with an **A** on the bottom.

As you'll see in the first two of the following chord frames, this is quite easy as all you have to do is lift your index finger off the **Bm(add11)** chord.

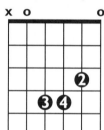

Bm(add11)   Bm(add11)/A

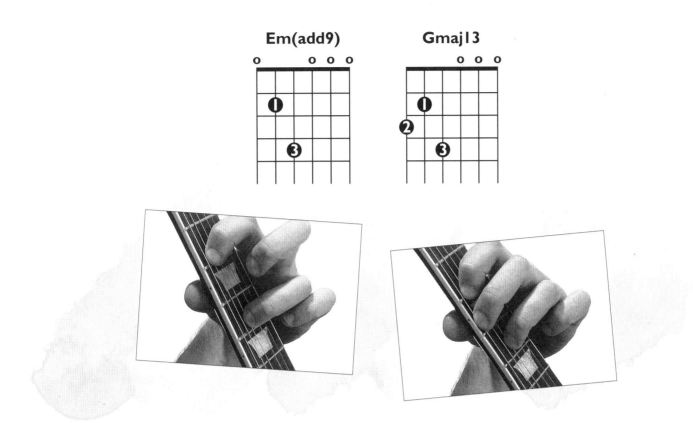

Em(add9)   Gmaj13

SAVE THE DRAMA FOR YOUR MAMA

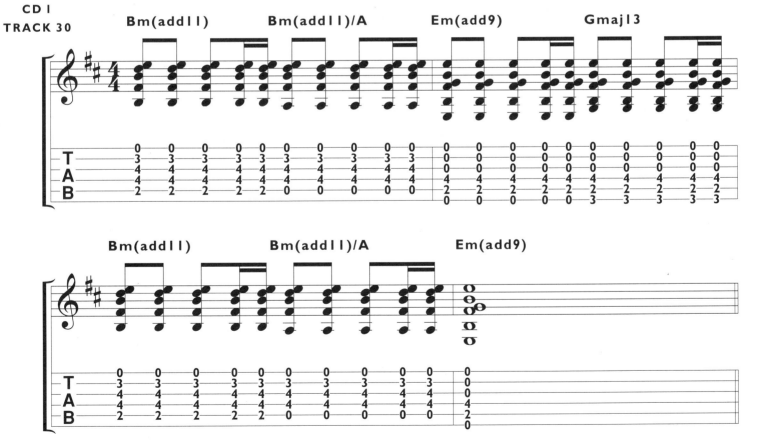

Let's try another group of new chords. Note that the bottom notes in the second and third chord boxes are fretted with the thumb, which is also used to mute the A string.

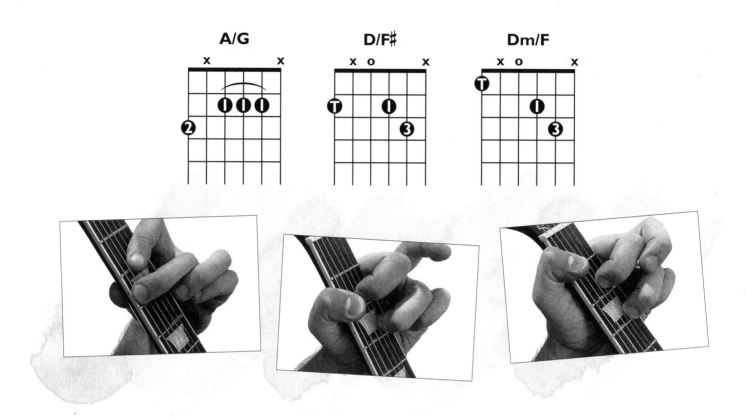

A/G   D/F#   Dm/F

IT'S LIKE DÉJÀ VU ALL OVER AGAIN

CD I
TRACK 31

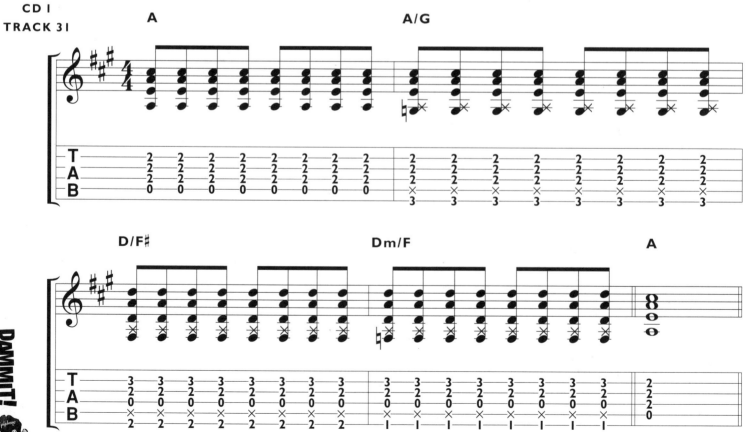

DAMMIT!

46

Before we go any further, let's try playing the following chord progression. You'll see that the chords used are the familiar *'Campfire Chords'* we covered in section **A**.

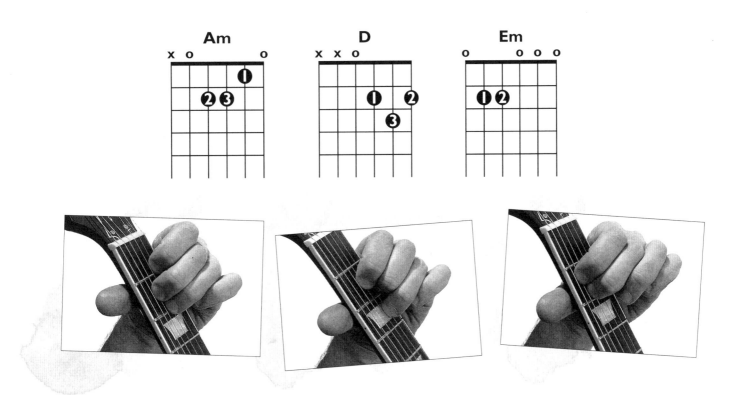

YAWN... BORING CHORDS

CD I
TRACK 32

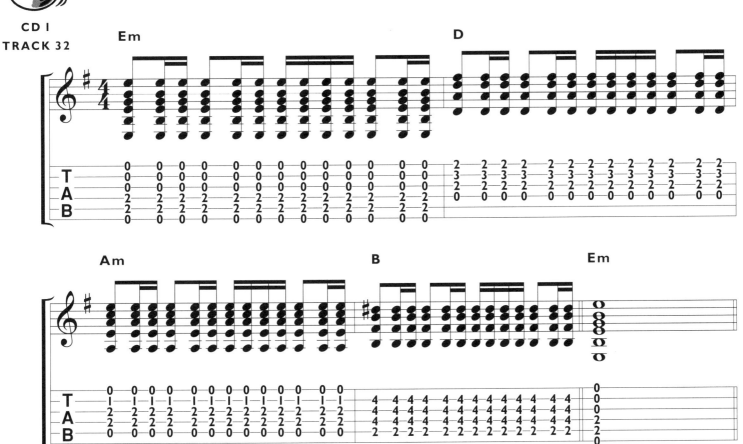

Now let's try dressing these plain, ordinary chords up a bit. We'll change the **E minor** to an **E minor 7th**, the **D** to a **Dadd$_{11}^{9}$**, the **A minor** to an **A minor 7th**, and the **B** to a nice, jazzy **B$_{\#9}^{\#5}$**.

(Although we already covered the **Dadd$_{11}^{9}$** chord in the previous section, I included it among these chord frames to illustrate how easy it is to slide from it into the next chord, the **Am7**.)

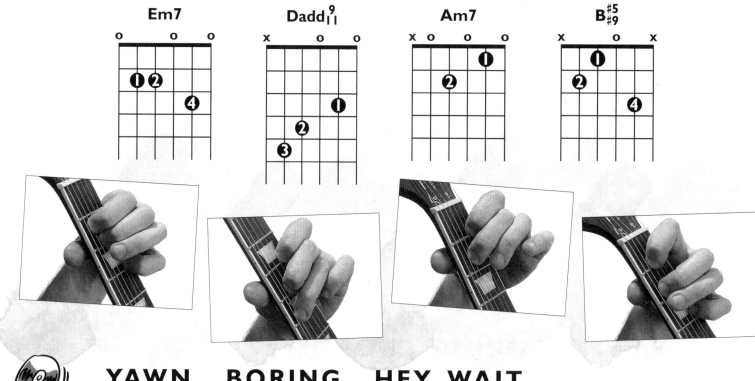

CD 1
TRACK 33

YAWN... BORING... HEY, WAIT, THIS IS KIND OF COOL

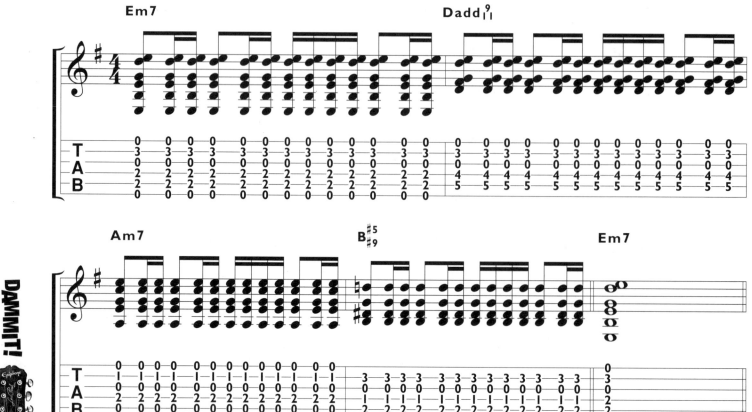

This next musical example features an alternate fingering for the **G major** chord (as shown in the last chord box).

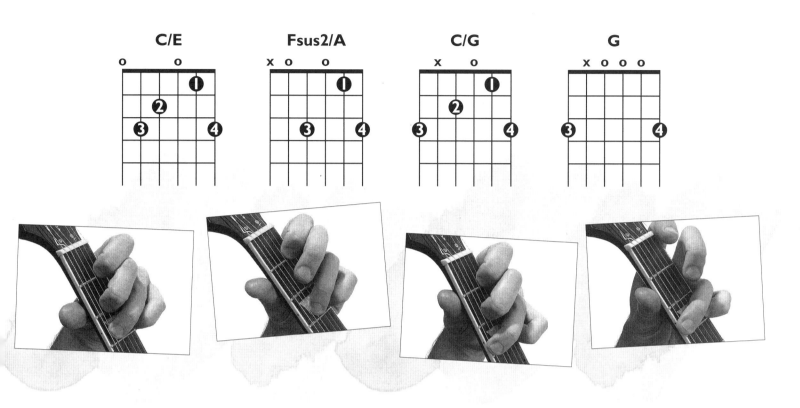

WE'VE GOT ALL YEAR

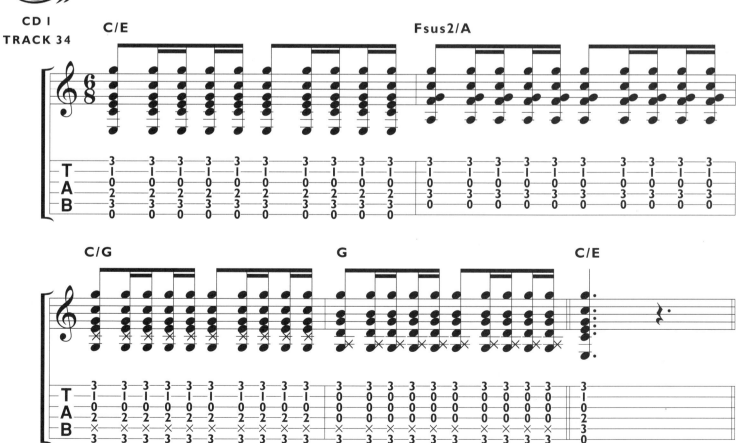

DRONE CHORDS

I love these. My first real spurt of development as a guitar player occurred when I learned how to incorporate open strings with fretted notes to create shimmering chords. I call these types of voicings drone chords because when they are played in any kind of sequence, the open strings are literally used as drones.

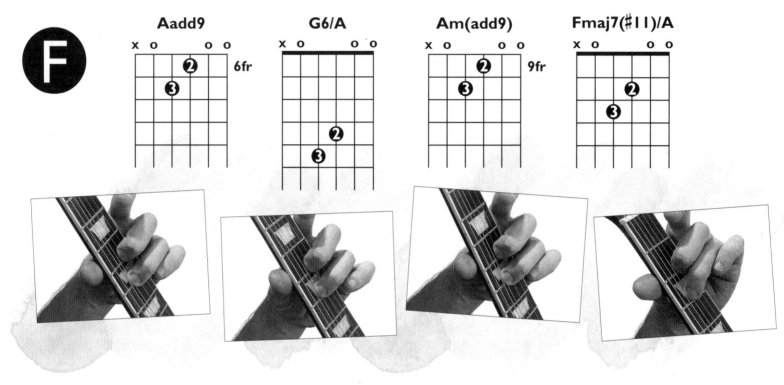

Aadd9   G6/A   Am(add9)   Fmaj7(#11)/A

HE JUST KEPT DRONING ON AND ON...

CD 1
TRACK 35

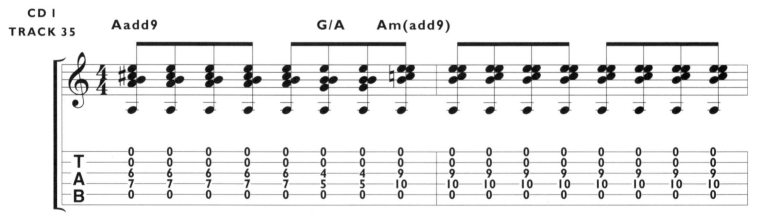

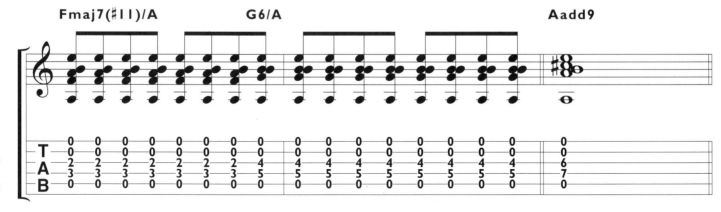

DAMMIT!

50

This first batch of chords uses the A, B and high E strings as drones; the only notes that change are those that are fretted on the D and G strings.

As you can see, one simple movable shape combined with open strings can produce four sophisticated-sounding yet ridiculously easy-to-play chords.

These two chords use the three high strings (G, B and E) as drones.

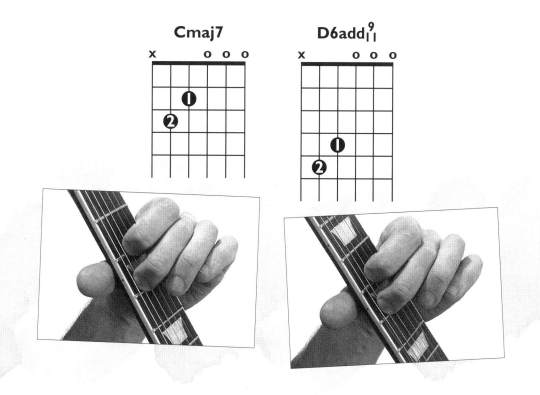

Cmaj7   D6add9/11

MOSH PIT IN THE DENTIST'S OFFICE

CD 1
TRACK 36

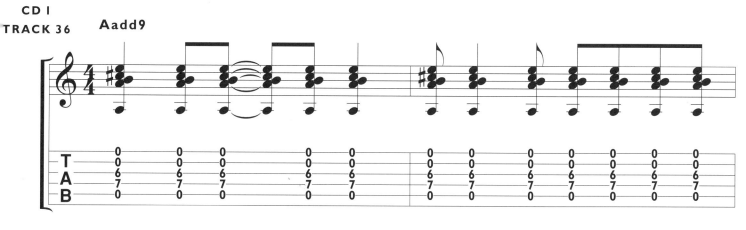

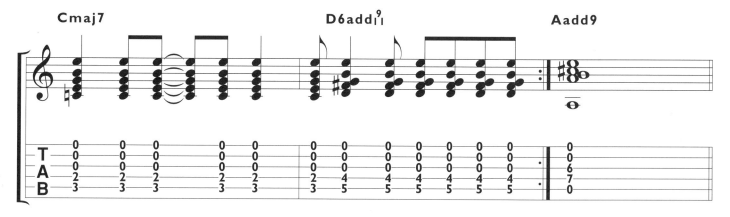

This group of drone chords is based on an ordinary **E major chord** (see section Ⓐ – *Campfire Chords*). Each one of these grips can simply be thought of as an **E chord** played at various locations on the fretboard, with the open low E and two open high strings ringing throughout.

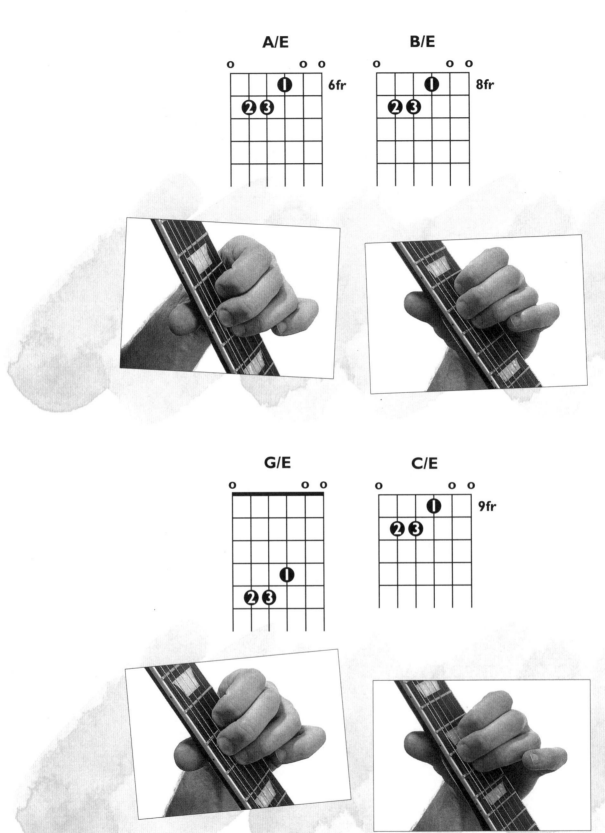

A/E

B/E

G/E

C/E

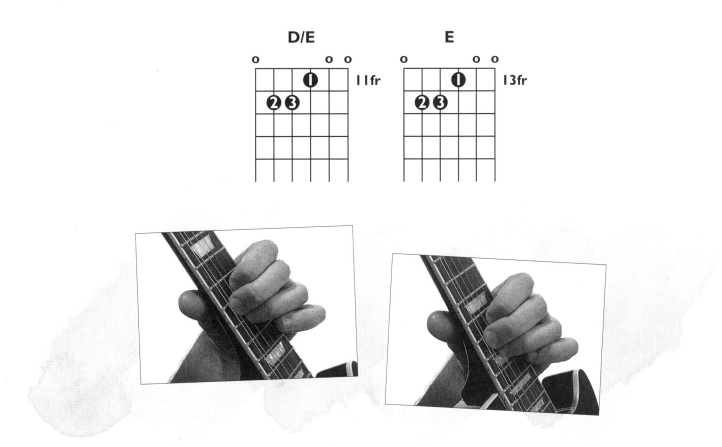

D/E   11fr   E   13fr

MANCHESTER ROCKS BUT GLOVERSVILLE SHAKES

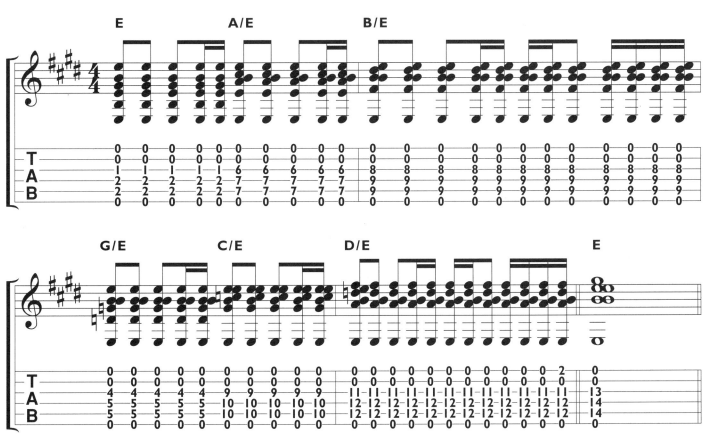

The following is similar to the group of chords we just covered in that the high B and E strings are again used as drones.

(Note that in the **C♯m7** chord, the G string is muted by the fourth finger.)

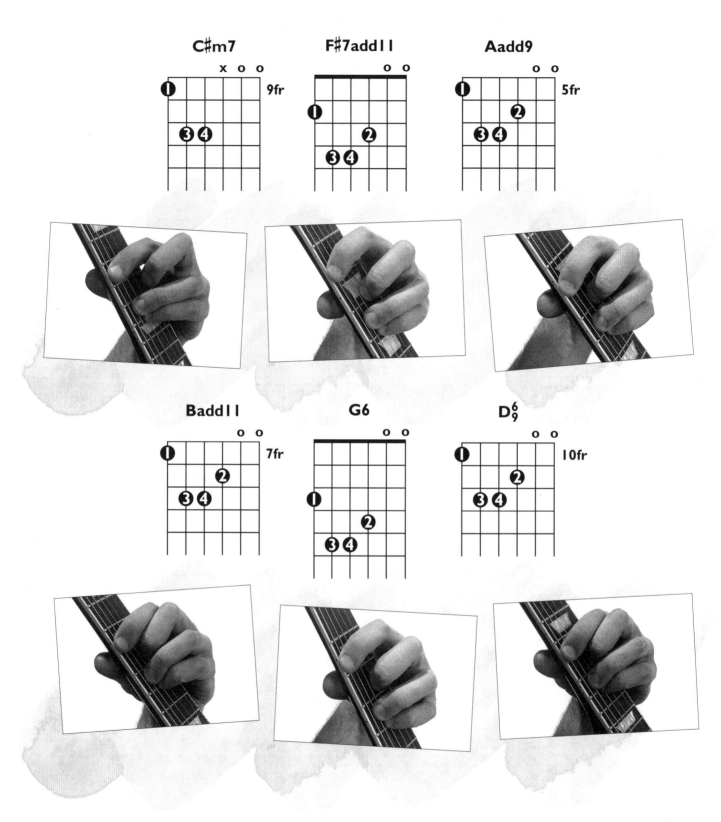

C♯m7   F♯7add11   Aadd9

Badd11   G6   D6/9

Obviously, I'm barely scratching the surface here. Given any of the six open strings to use as drones combined with any number of movable chord shapes available to you, the possibilities are mind-boggling. Use your imagination… who knows what you might come up with.

CD 1
TRACK 38

WHERE DID I PUT THOSE MAJESTIC SUPERSONIC PUMPKINS?

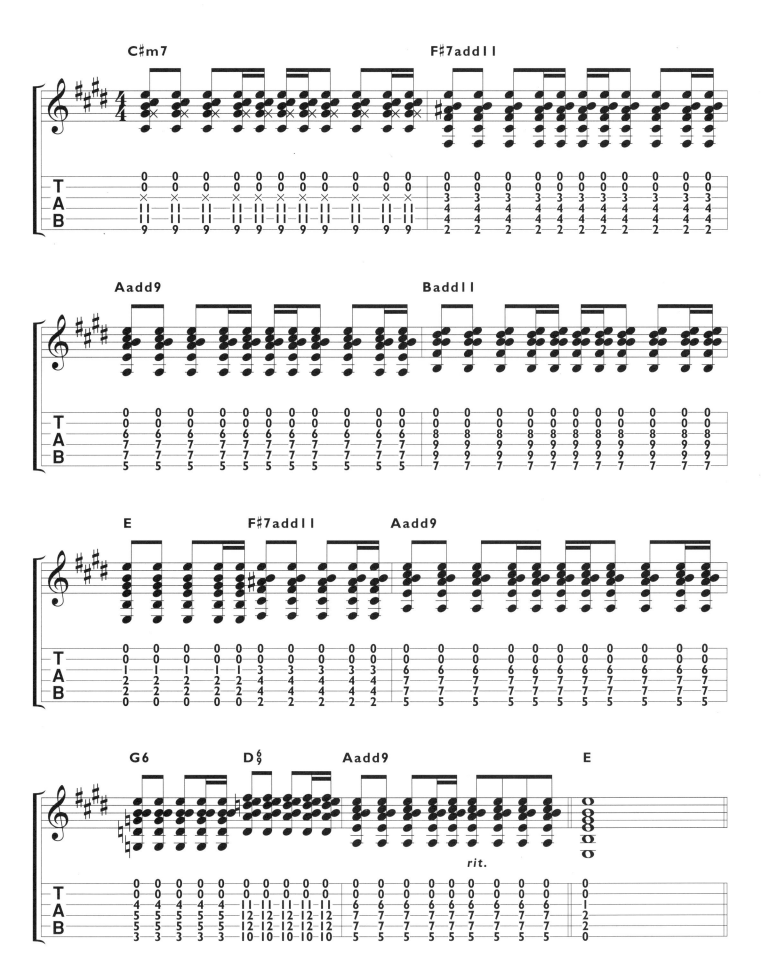

JAZZY CHORDS

These chords won't necessarily turn you into the next Pat Metheny, but they can break you out of the ordinary major/minor rut. Try throwing some of these in when you want to spice things up a little… they'll work in any context, be it jazz (obviously), rock, folk or just about any style of music you can think of (okay, maybe not punk).

JAZZ SCHMAZZ

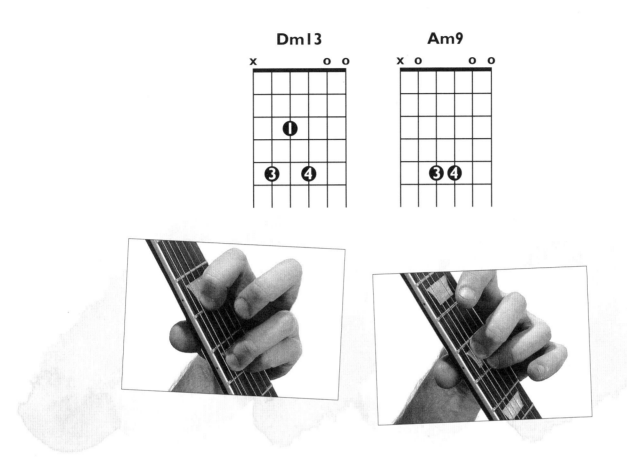

WALTZING ON WATER

Fortunately, jazz-flavoured chords such as **7ths**, **9ths**, **11ths**, **13ths** and even **7♯9s** can all be played as movable shapes!

This is a movable **7th** shape. With this, you'll be able to play any **7th** chord you want without having to change finger positions.

KEVIN'S SEVENTH HEAVEN

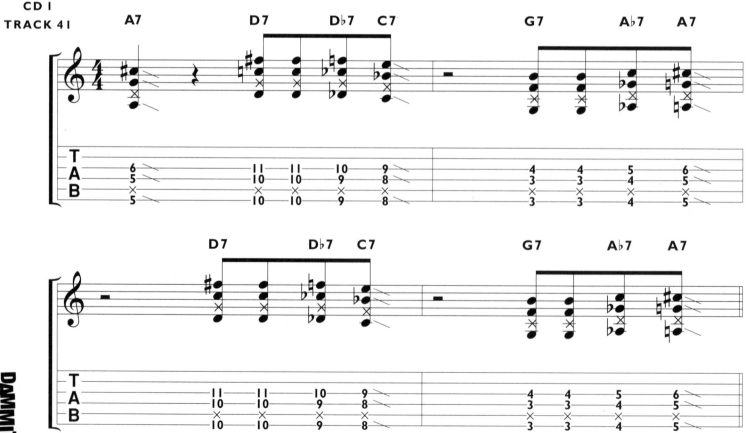

Here we have a movable **9th**.

TALKIN' MOVABLE BLUES #9

CD I
TRACK 42

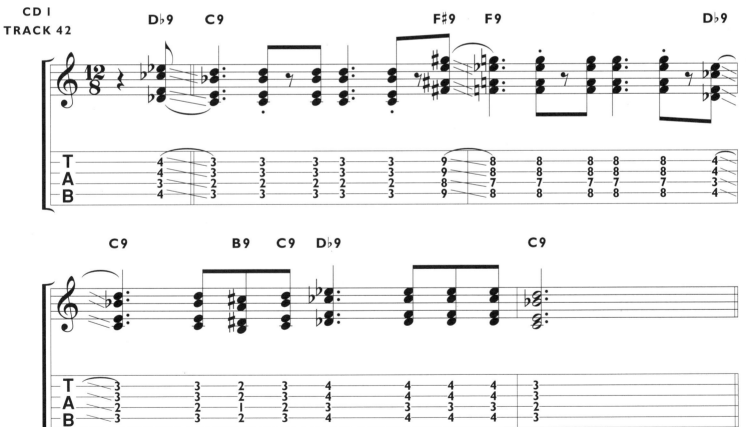

This **11th** chord shape requires only one finger. Could it possibly get any simpler?

SMOOTH LIKE ME

CD I
TRACK 43

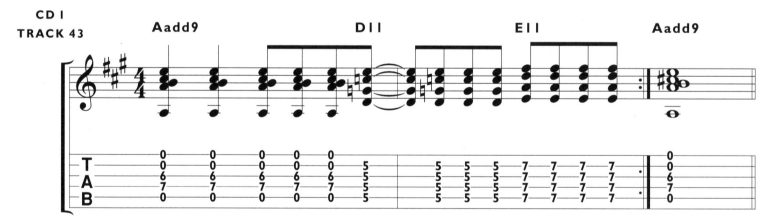

Master this movable **13th** shape and you can start referring to other musicians as 'cats.'

CD I
TRACK 44

BAD LUCK THEME FOR CATS
WHO PLAY 13THS

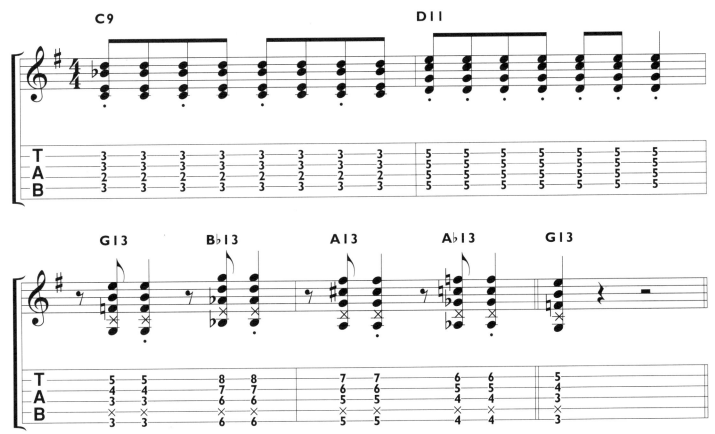

We'll conclude with the **7 9 chord** ('7 sharp 9'), also sometimes affectionately referred to as the *'Purple ♯Haze'* chord. Here are two different ways to play it.

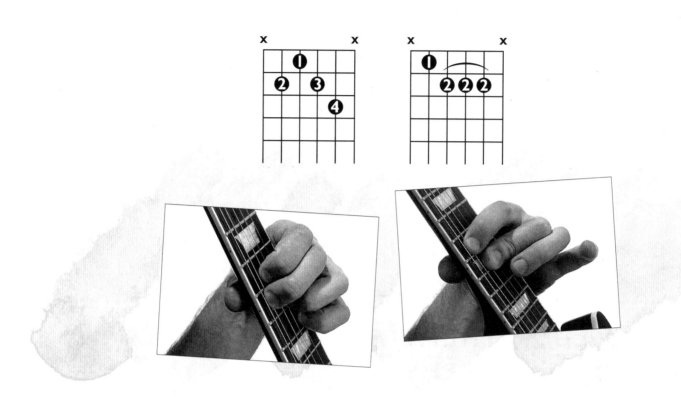

THESE JAZZ CHORDS ROCK

CD I
TRACK 45

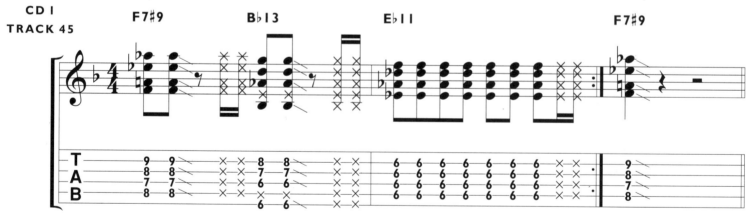

THANK YOU VERY MUCH, GOOD NIGHT (AGAIN)

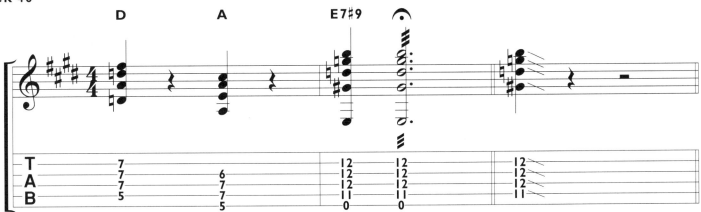

POWER CHORDS

There are some in our society who will claim that Western civilisation began a steady decline when these simple little confections began creeping into popular music in the 1950s. The sound of this chord has inspired multitudes to pick up a guitar (or tennis racket) and summon the rock. Indeed, there's nothing quite like a good old-fashioned power chord cranked to 11 to get the blood boiling.

Virtually all power chords are movable; here are four that are played in the open position.

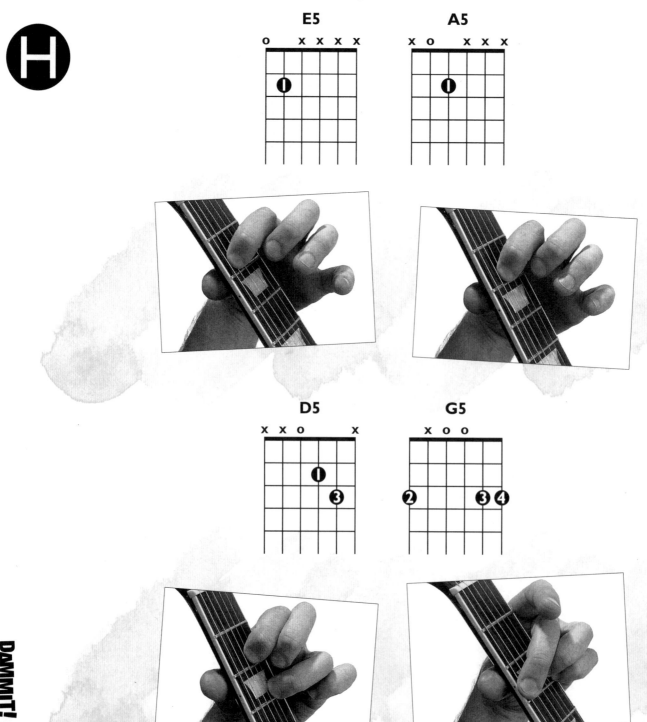

The following are basic movable power chord shapes. I believe the one in the first box is easier to fret so while I favour it, I have included the second type as well since you will most likely come across it in other guitar publications.

And there you have it. Without further ado… let's get to the music.

HÄIR POWËR

CD I
TRACK 47

PÖWER BÄLLAD

CD I
TRACK 48

UMLAUTS ARE FÜN

CD I
TRACK 49

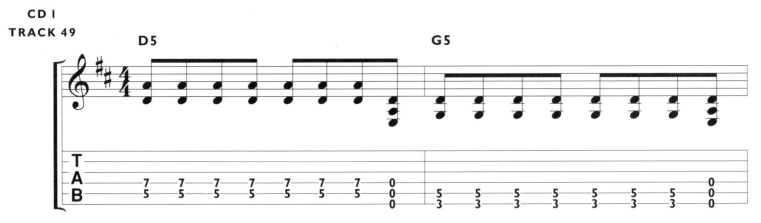

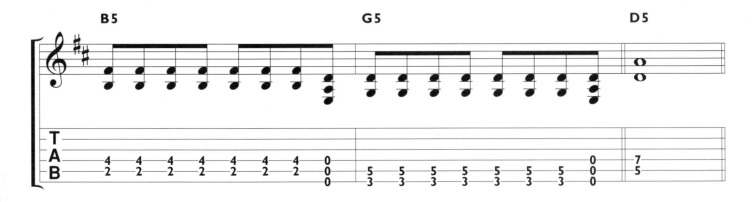

Some of these riffs use power chords with the root on either the fifth or sixth string. Using both often saves you from having to move too far up the neck.

 CALIPUNK

CD 1
TRACK 50

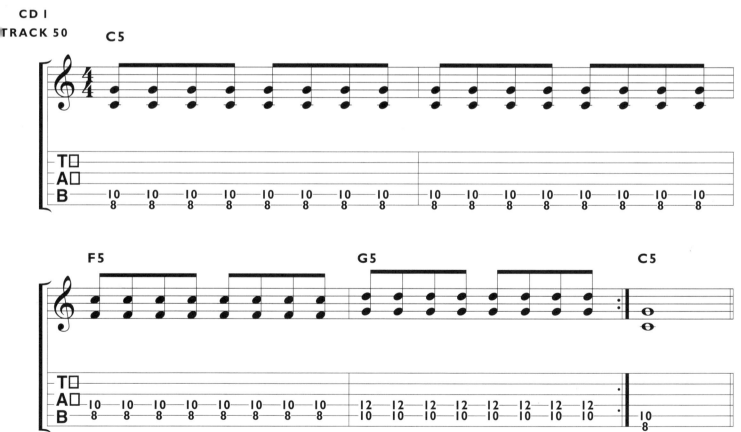

Remember, you can thicken the sound of any '5' chord by adding the octave with your little finger. The fifth and octave will *always* sound good with overdrive!

DON'T HAVE A COW

CD 1
TRACK 51

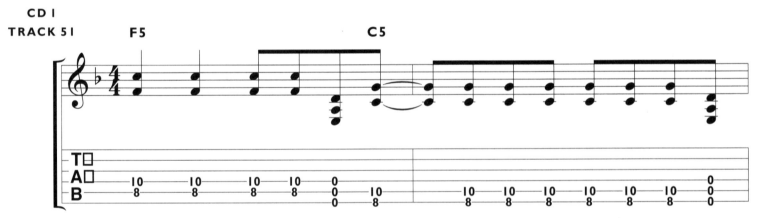

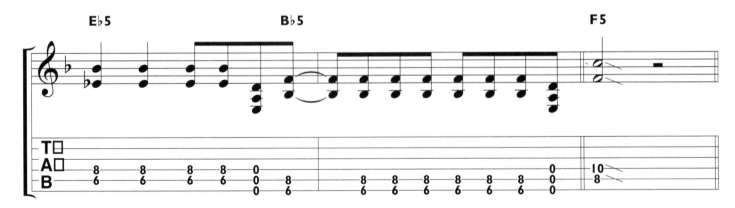

68

This musical snippet is played using palm mutes (P. M.). Rest the meaty part of your picking hand (the outside edge) across the strings near the bridge (but don't press too hard), then crank up the distortion and let 'er rip.

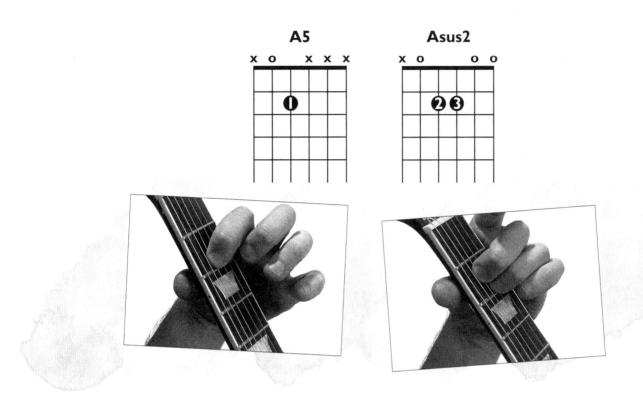

POWDER POP

CD 1
TRACK 52

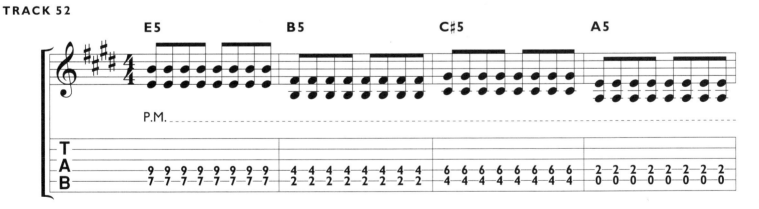

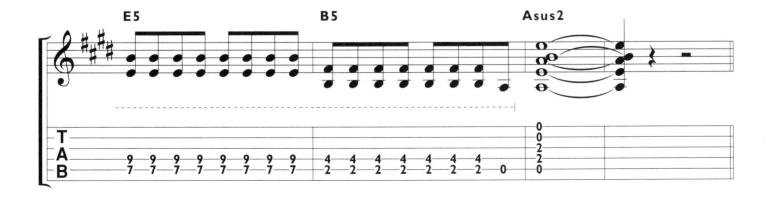

This last musical example contains a common pattern often credited to Chuck Berry. It requires an alternate fingering for the standard power chord, plus another movable shape that doesn't really have a proper name; I call it the **power sixth**.

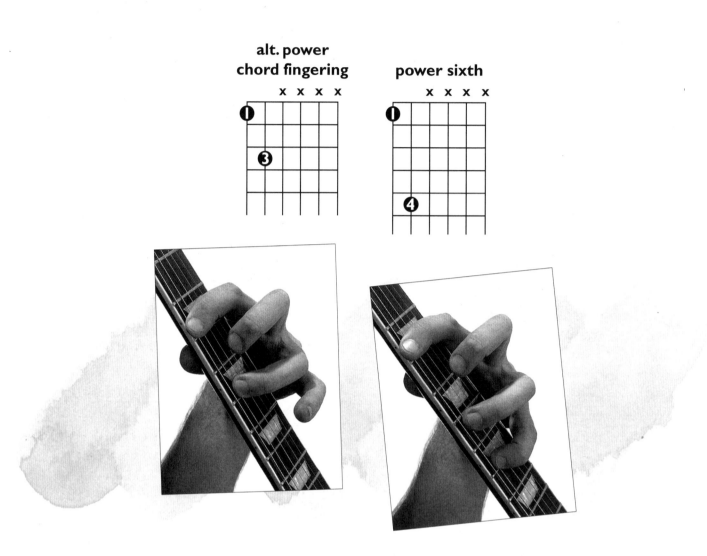

alt. power
chord fingering   power sixth

BOOGIE UPSIDE YOUR HEAD

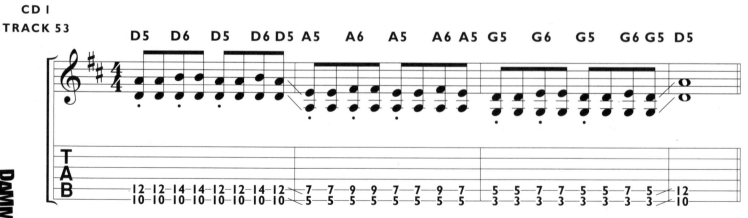

PLAY SOLOS

PLAY SOLOS

You're on stage, the singer has just finished the second chorus of the song, and all eyes are now on you. It's time to deliver the rock; so what are you going to play now, hotshot?

The number one misconception about lead guitar is that it has to be *fast*. No less a guitar legend than Mountain's Leslie West has often stated that lead guitar playing is all about tone, bending and vibrato. When I was a kid listening to bands like Bad Company and Pink Floyd, it never occurred to me that their respective guitarists, Mick Ralphs and David Gilmour, were actually not that 'flashy' from a technical standpoint; this was because their leads were so damn *tasty* that their lack of speed escaped me. To this day, that single bend at the end of each chorus of Bad Company's *'Rock Steady'* just *kills* me every time I hear it. One simple note, played with an attitude.

So with all due respect to Messrs. Van Halen (who, by the way, happens to play some very fine melodic lines underneath all the flash), Rhoads, Dimebag Darrell, Vai, Malmsteen and Blackmore, I now submit to you 25 tried-and-true rock licks that anyone can play.

I've loosely arranged the licks in order of difficulty; due to varying skill levels, some of you may disagree with the sequence. That's okay... feel free to skip around as needed. Also, each one of these licks is on the CD; you may wish to listen to how it's played first, *then* play along. In all cases, if you have any difficulty, just practice the lick in question *slowly*. Keep in mind as well that all of these licks may appear or sound to some listeners much more difficult than they actually are.

HEY, THESE AREN'T SO HARD

Let's start with an easy blues-based one in A. Remember: *attitude* will more than make up for any lack of 'chops.'

CD I
TRACK 54

LICK I

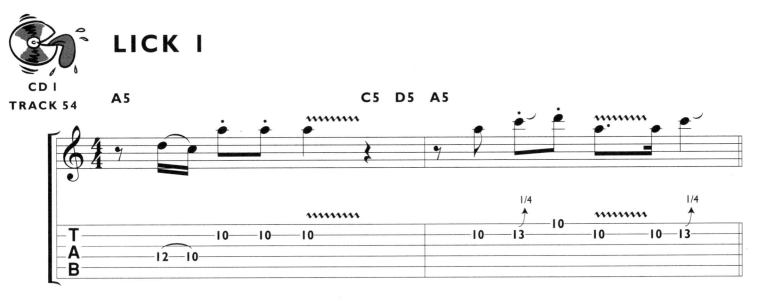

The lick in the last bar of this next example works really well as a bluegrass ending. Yee haw.

CD I
TRACK 55

LICK 2

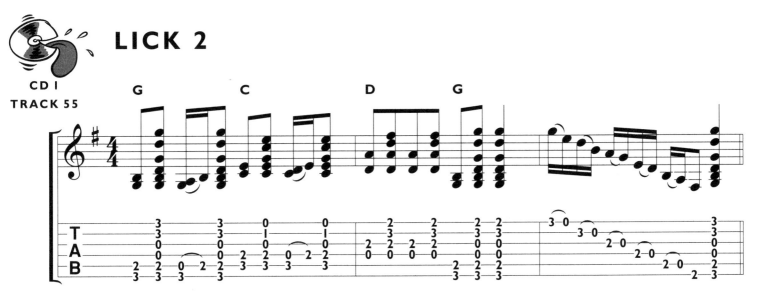

Whoever said "the faster it is, the better" obviously doesn't possess the *funk*.

LICK 3

CD 1
TRACK 56

Here's a major pentatonic lick for a bright, sunny day. Dig into those bends and make 'em sing.

LICK 4

CD 1
TRACK 57

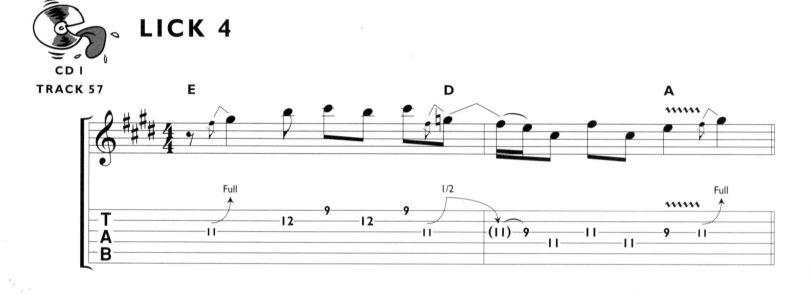

It's all about soul...

LICK 5

CD 1
TRACK 58

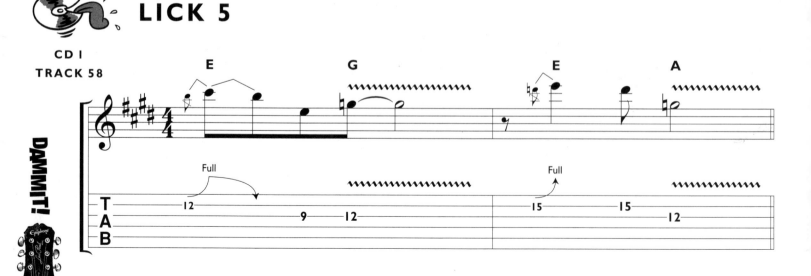

LICK 6

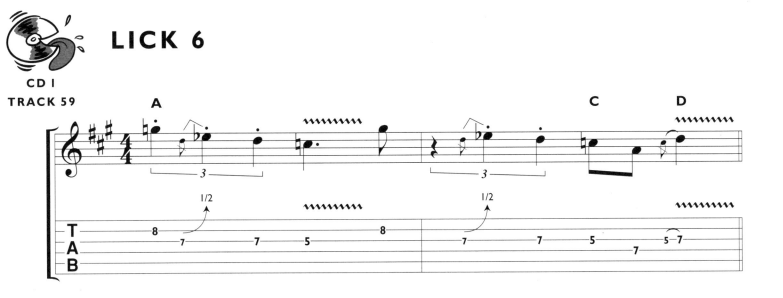

LICK 7

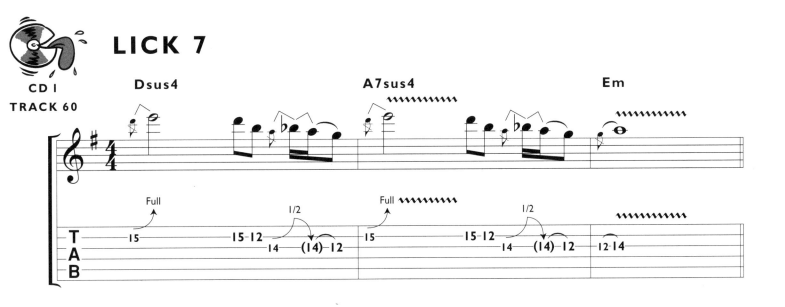

Here's another slow, funky one. Check out the wide one-and-a-half step bend in the second bar, and be sure to play it in tune!

LICK 8

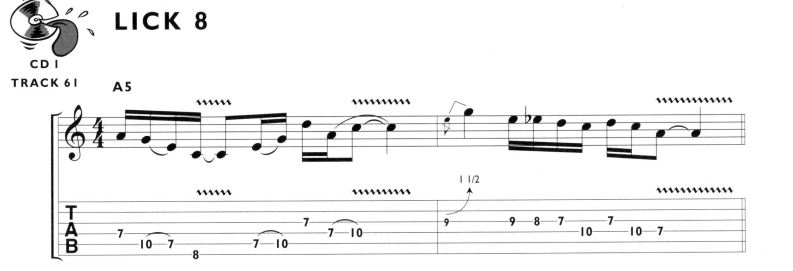

Project a truckload of soul without having to bend even a single note.

LICK 9

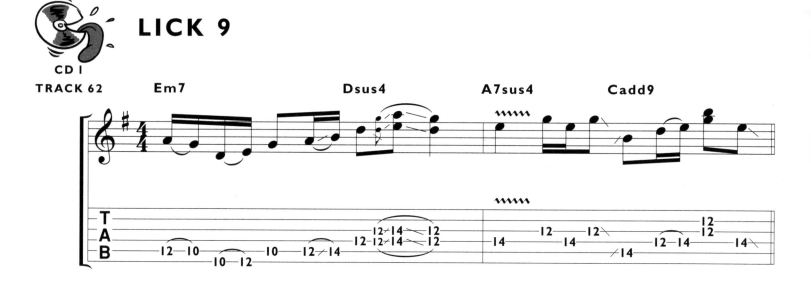

The lick in the second bar of this jazzy phrase is actually the same as the one in the first, played three frets higher.

LICK 10

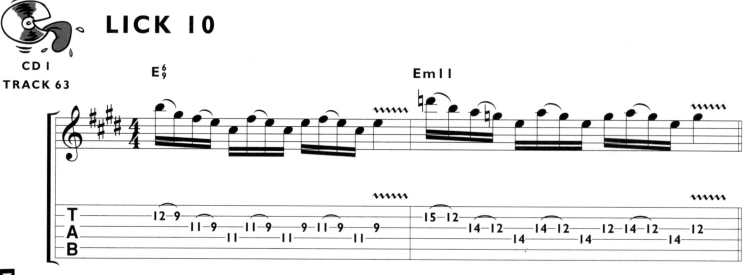

OH, THESE AREN'T QUITE AS EASY AS THE OTHER ONES

Do not fear, though… they're still not that bad. We'll begin with another bluegrass-inspired lick.

LICK 11

CD I
TRACK 64

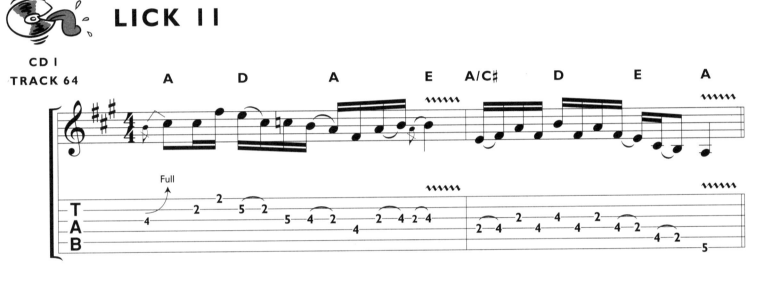

This group of licks is standard-issue **A minor** pentatonic riffage.

LICK 12

CD I
TRACK 65

LICK 13

A5

LICK 14

A5

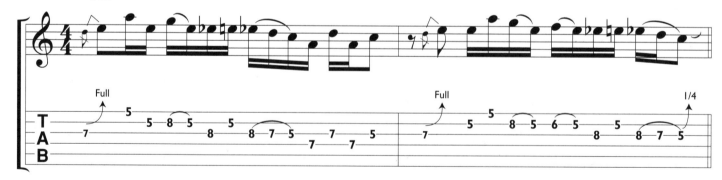

This one uses an **E minor** pentatonic pattern.

LICK 15

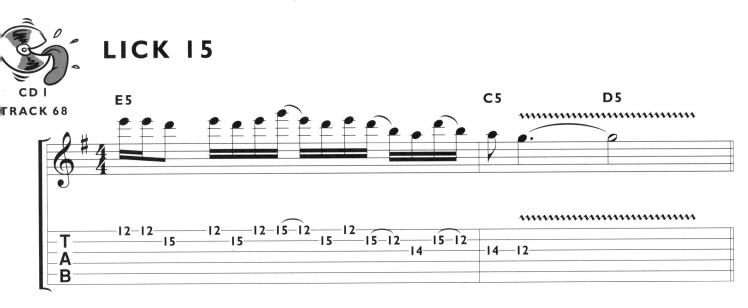

The fact that you're soloing doesn't mean you have to be playing the *whole* time.
This phrase makes use of rests, or pauses, to make the licks themselves stand out
more.

LICK 16

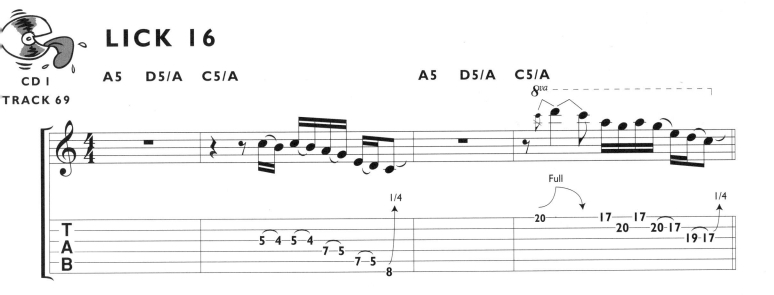

The trickiness of this lick has very little to do with speed and a lot to do with timing.

LICK 17

CD 1
TRACK 70

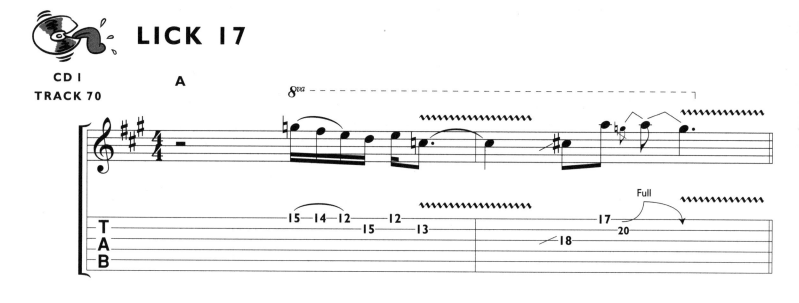

Speed is not really an issue with this one, either. Dig into each note, especially in the second bar, and try to play as though you are singing through your instrument.

LICK 18

CD 1
TRACK 71

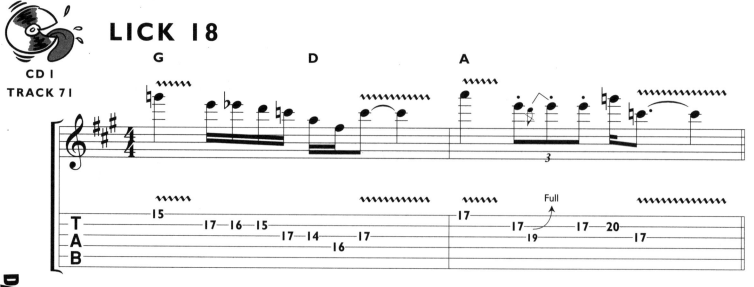

LICK 19

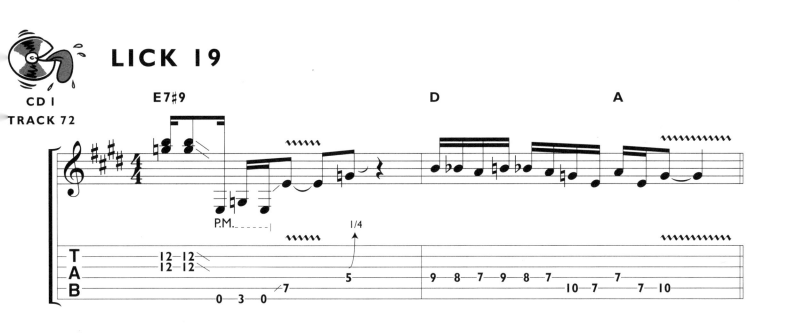

LICK 20

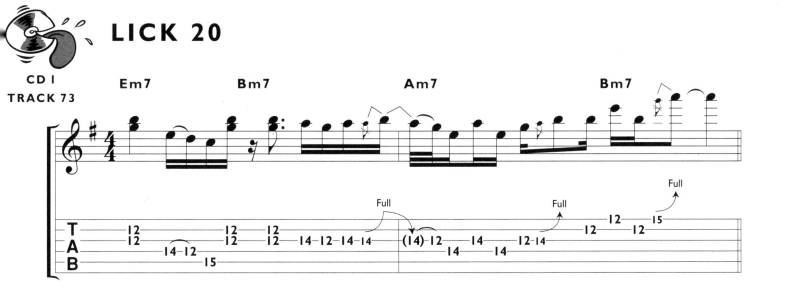

REPEATING HEAD-TURNER LICKS

When I'm on stage and I'm stuck for an idea in the middle of a solo, I pull out one of these. I don't know why, but audiences just seem to go crazy when you play a fast lick over and over again. So what if the lick isn't hard to execute? Well, the audience certainly doesn't need to know that. Just make a tortured face and act like you're working harder than you are.

Don't be scared off by the musical notation in our first lick. As you can see, the whole thing is done with fret hand pulloffs, so your pick hand actually has very little work to do.

LICK 21

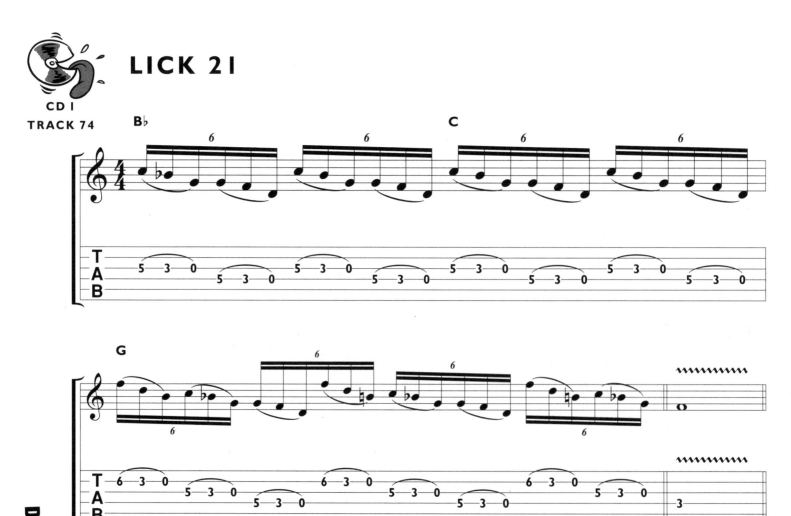

This one resolves itself with a simple phrase in the second bar.

LICK 22

CD I
TRACK 75

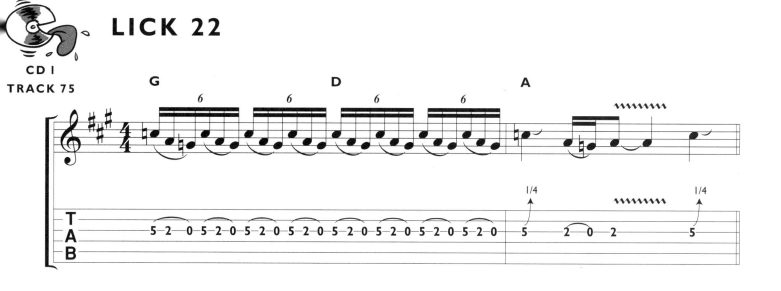

Try these out when you need to get yourself unstuck.

LICK 23

CD I
TRACK 76

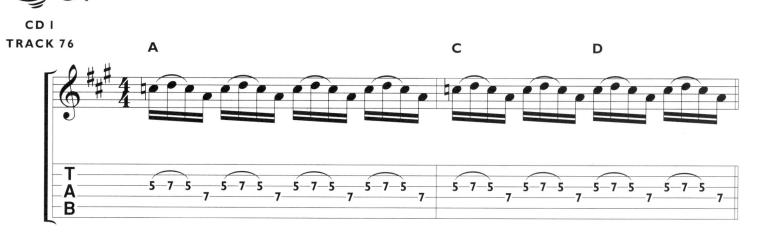

LICK 24

CD I
TRACK 77

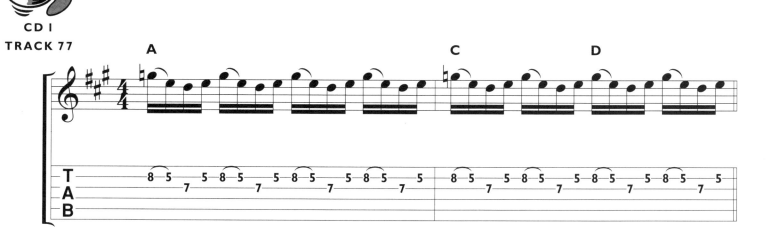

Ah, the motherlode. This one should melt the hearts and eardrums of
Lynyrd Skynyrd and Led Zeppelin fans alike.

LICK 25

CD 1
TRACK 78

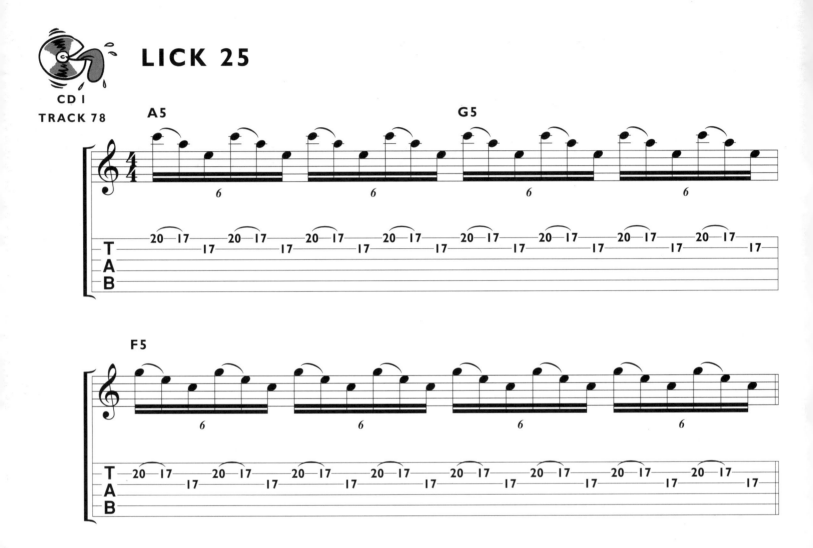

What better way to close this book than to put everything we've learned into practice?

Throughout the following section, we'll cover three popular styles of music:
reggae, funk blues and rock. Each of the four songs featured contains two guitar parts:
one rhythm and one lead.

Enjoy!

STYLES

TIE-DYED PIZZA KEG

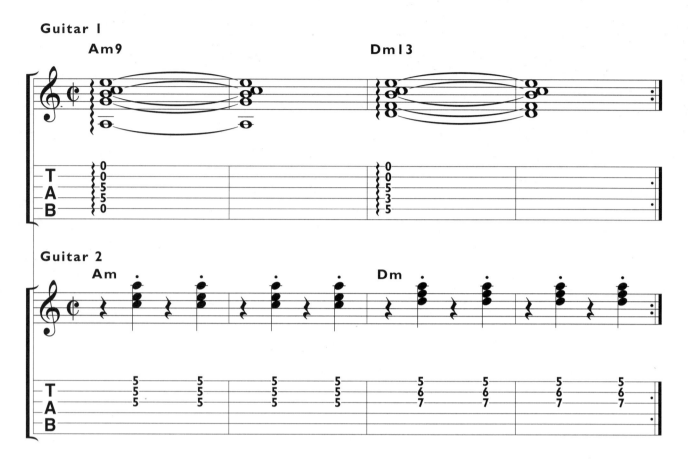

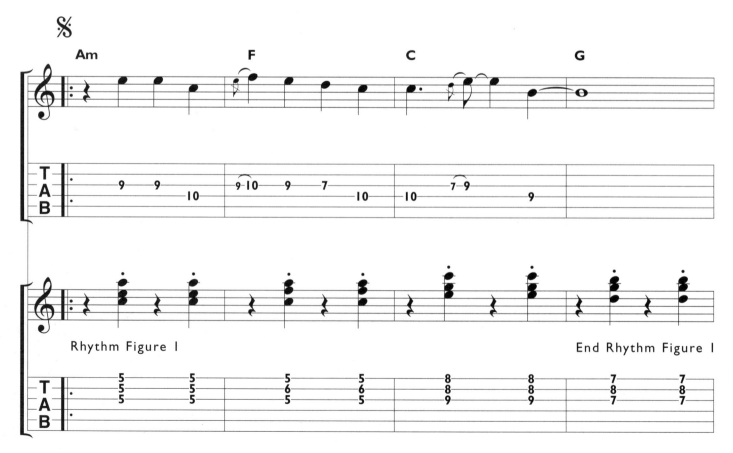

86

Guitar I

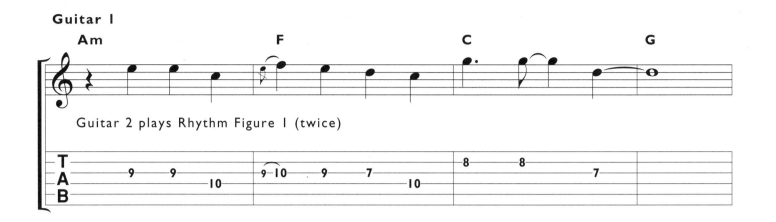

Guitar 2 plays Rhythm Figure I (twice)

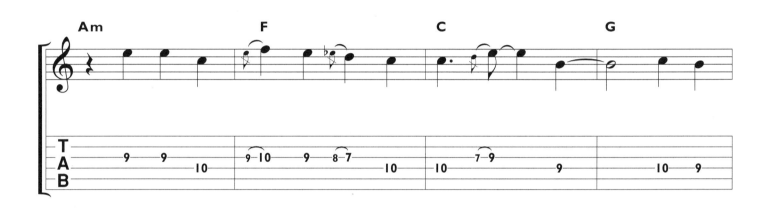

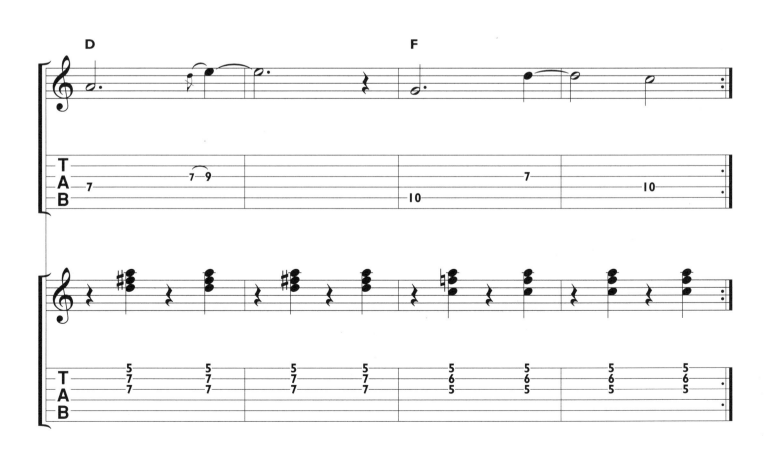

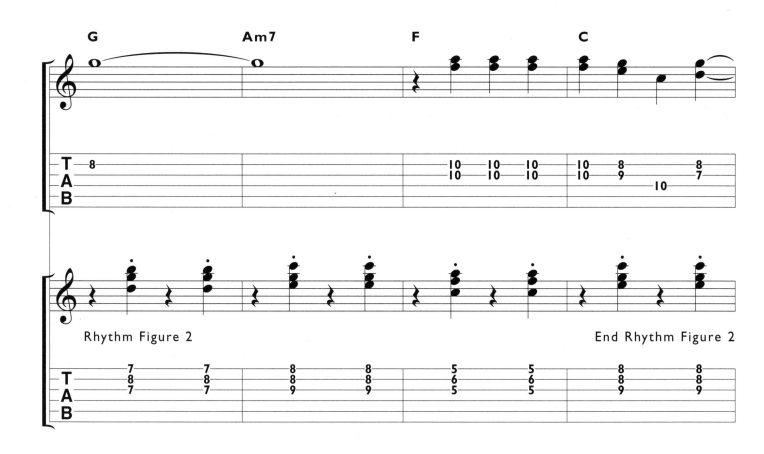

Rhythm Figure 2

End Rhythm Figure 2

Guitar 1

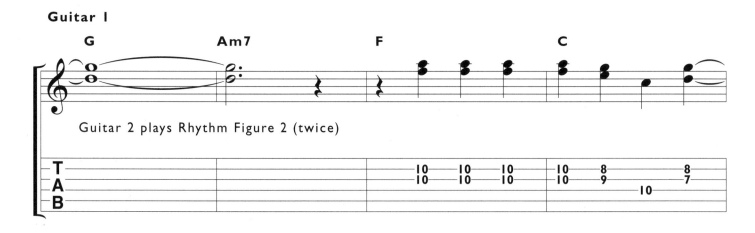

Guitar 2 plays Rhythm Figure 2 (twice)

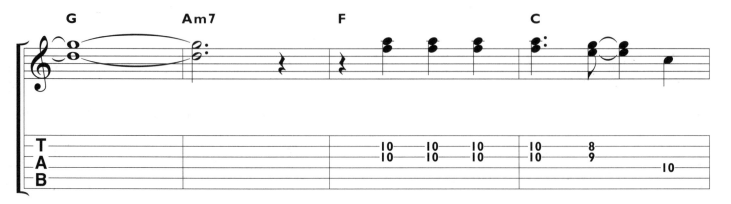

Guitar 1

D.S. al Coda
(no repeat)

Guitar 2

⊕ Coda

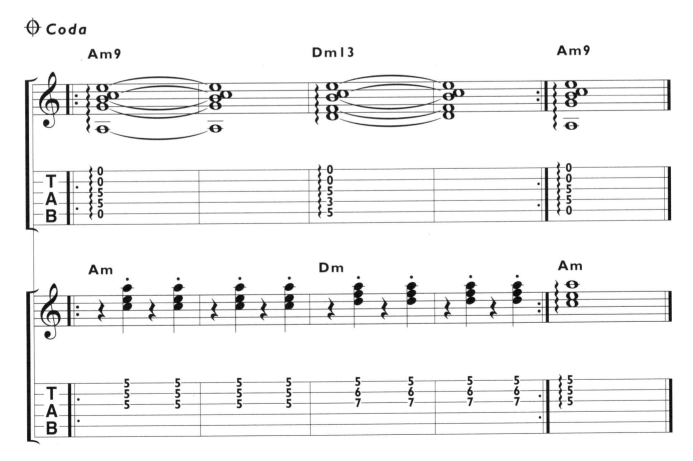

CD 1
TRACK 81

THAT WASN'T CHICKEN

TRACK 82
*Backing Track
Without*
**LEAD
GUITAR**

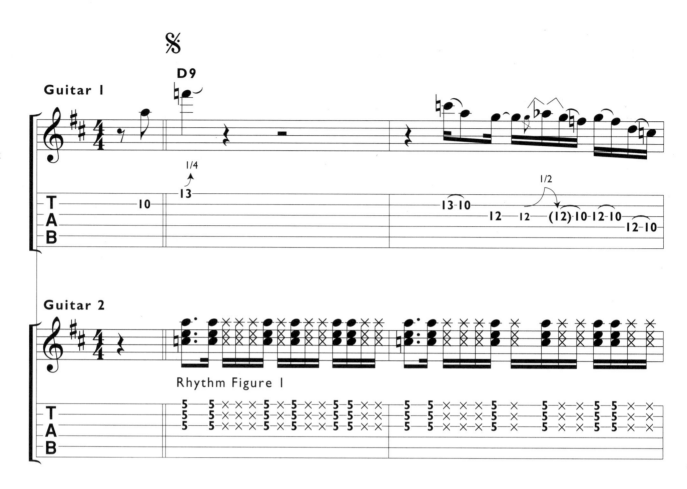

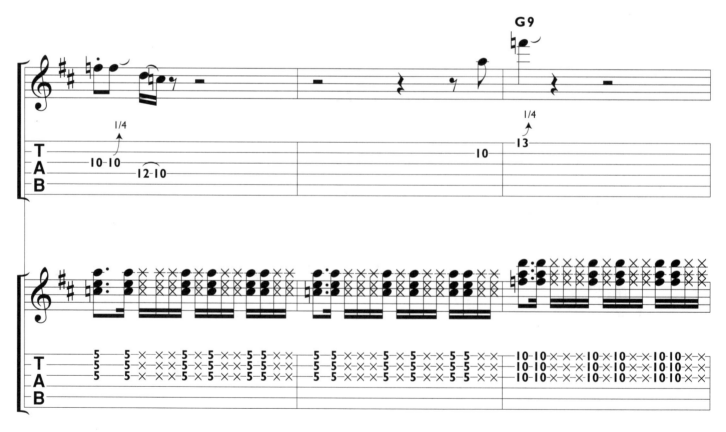

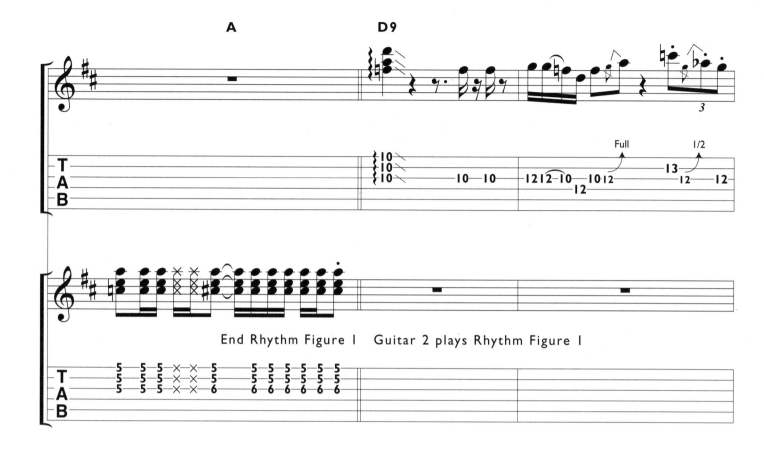

End Rhythm Figure 1   Guitar 2 plays Rhythm Figure 1

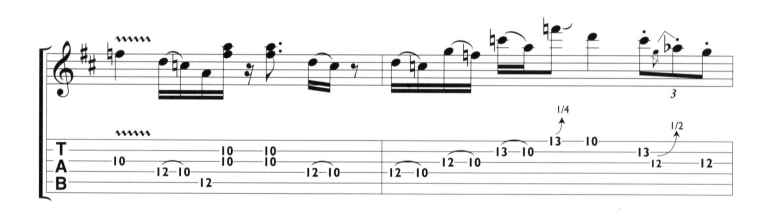

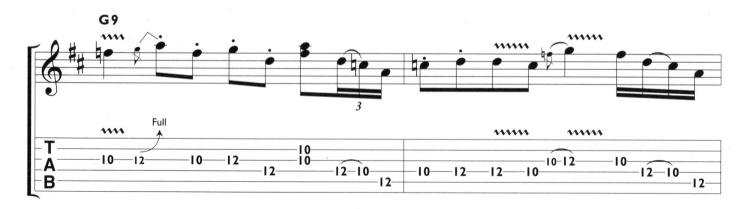

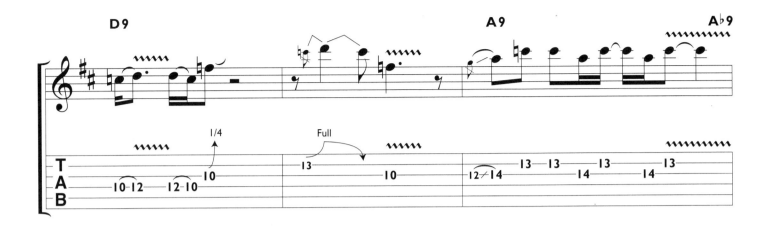

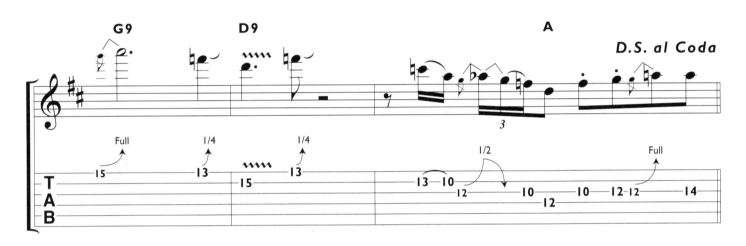

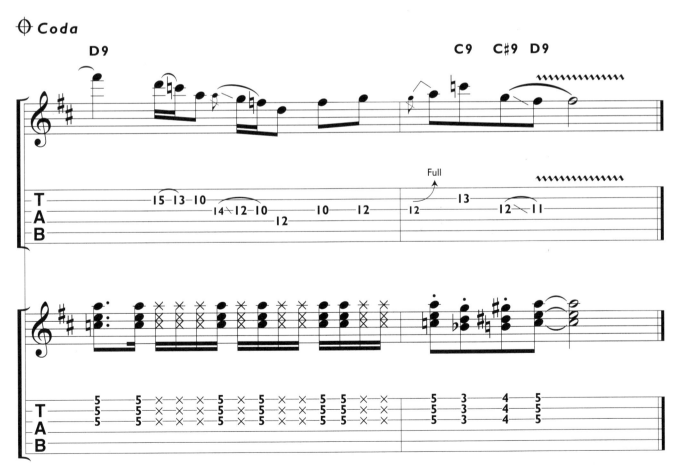

CD 1
TRACK 83

IT AIN'T GONNA FIT IN THERE

TRACK 84
Backing Track
Without
LEAD
GUITAR

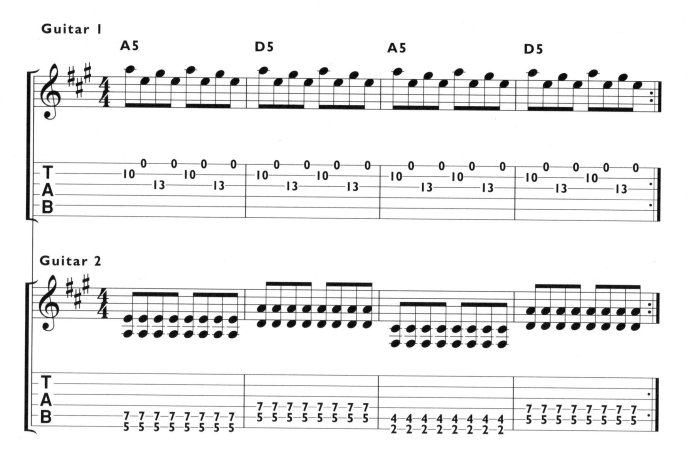

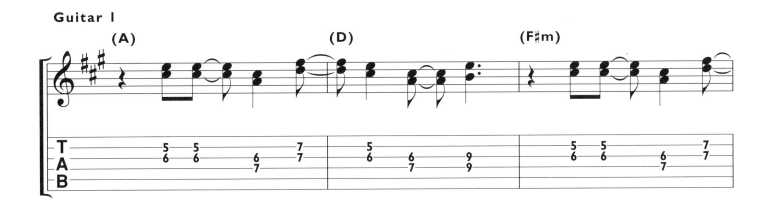

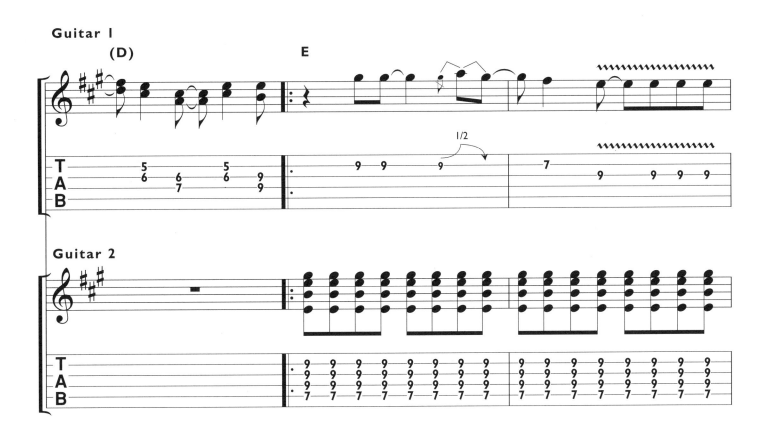

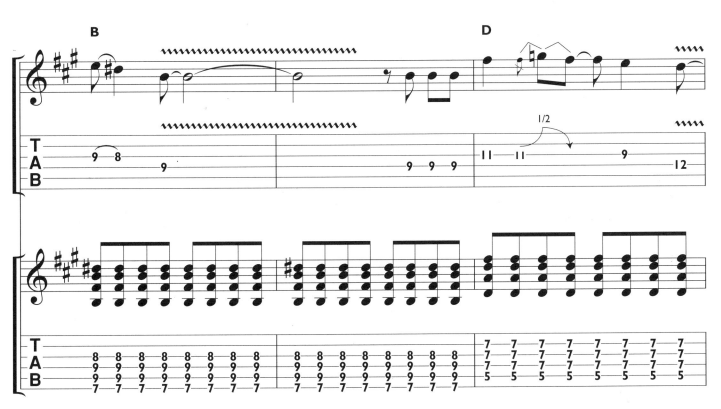

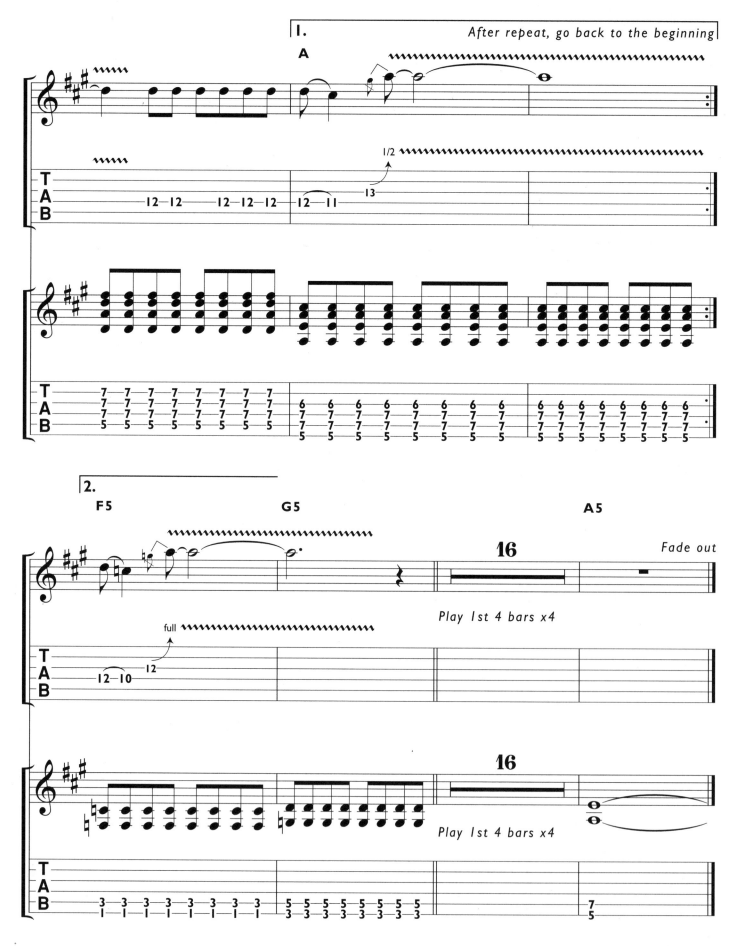

FUNKLY MY DEAR

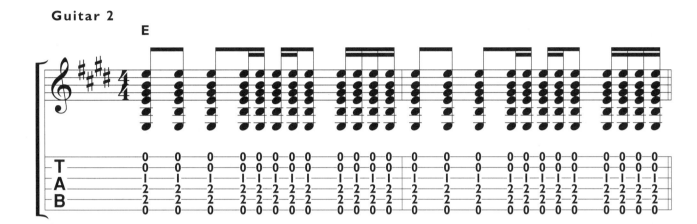

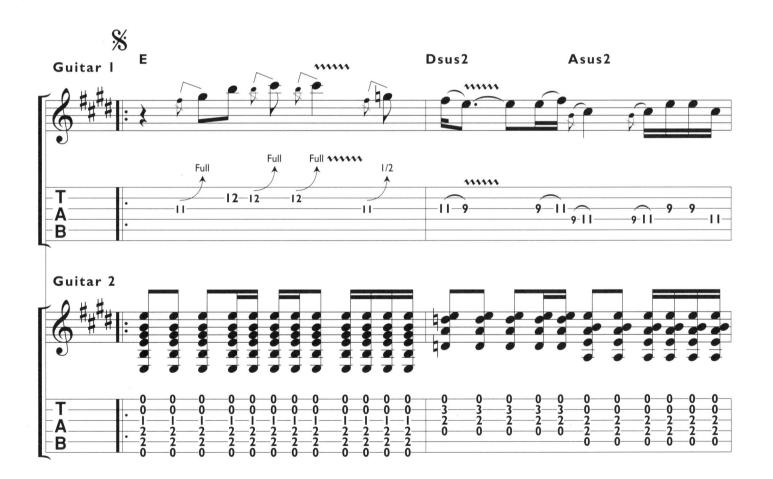

97

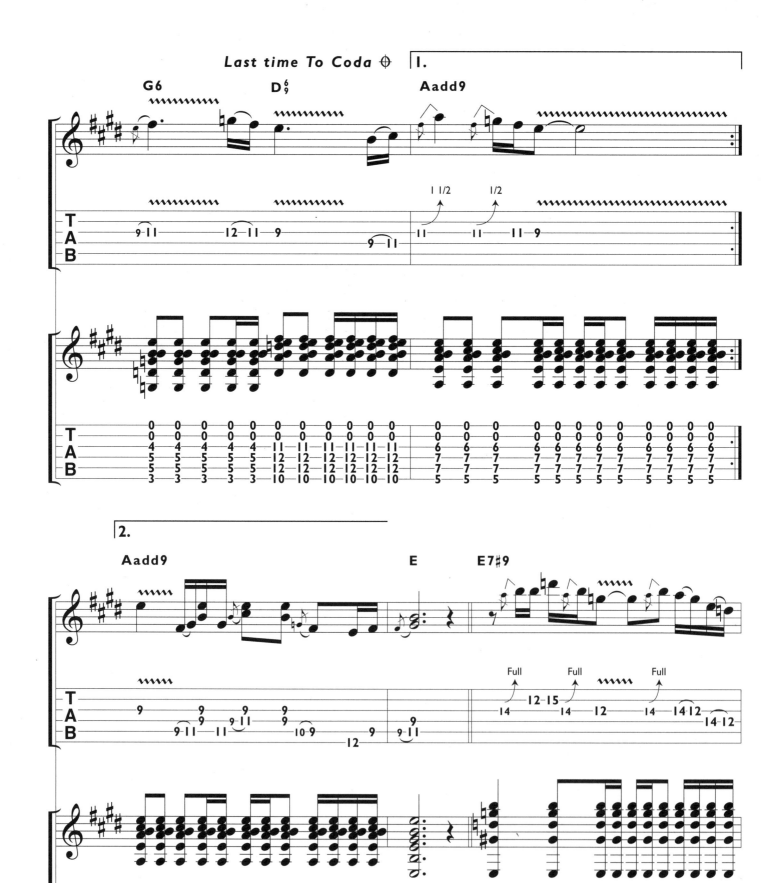

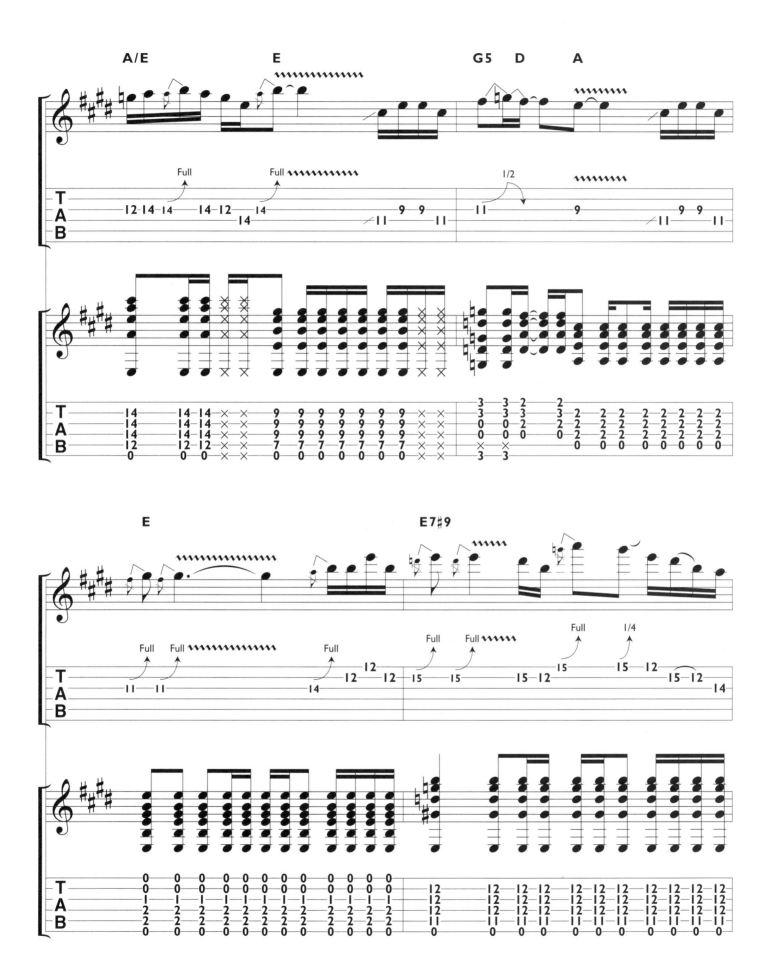

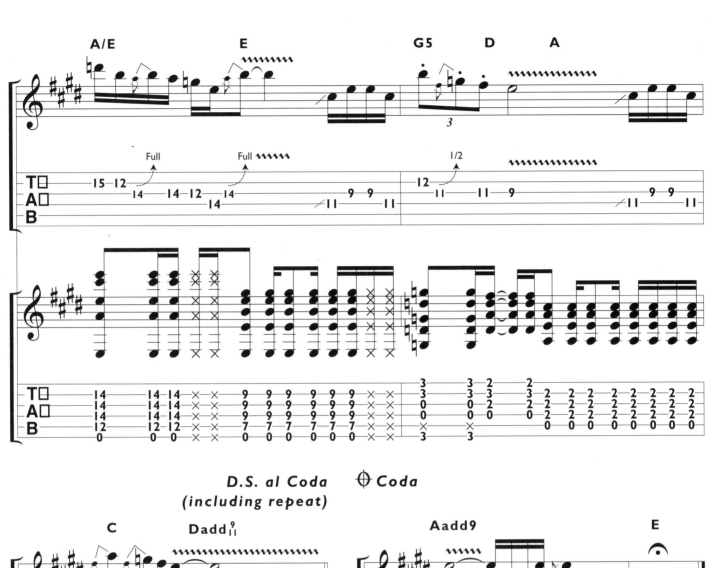

D.S. al Coda
(including repeat)   ⊕ **Coda**

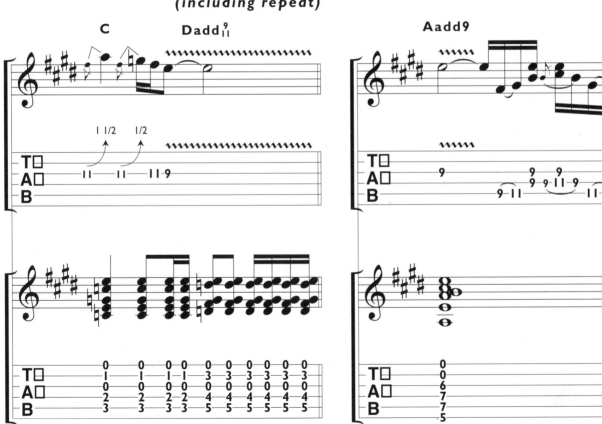

BONUS SONGS

CD 2
TRACK 1

TRACK 2
Without
**RHYTHM
GUITAR**

TRACK 3
Without
**LEAD
GUITAR**

THE HOUSE OF THE RISING SUN

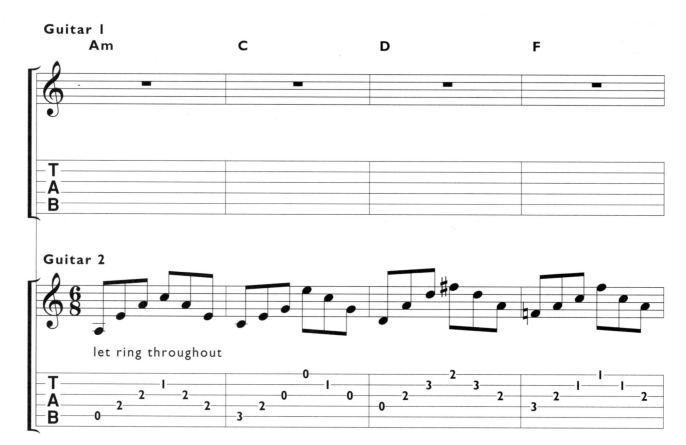

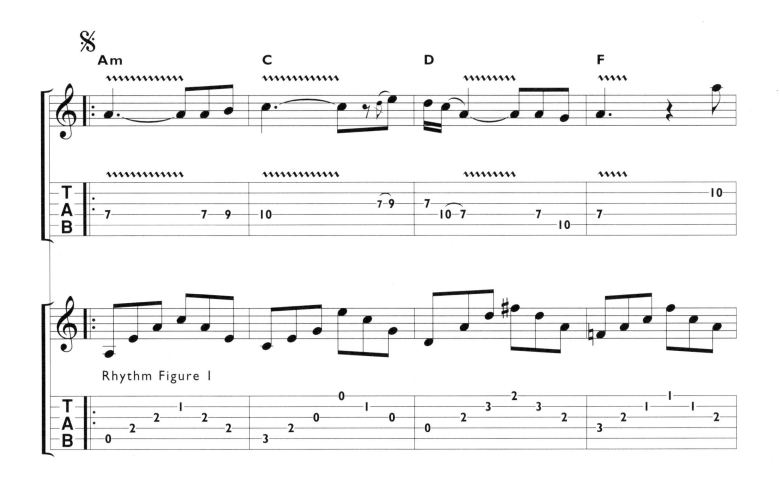

Rhythm Figure I

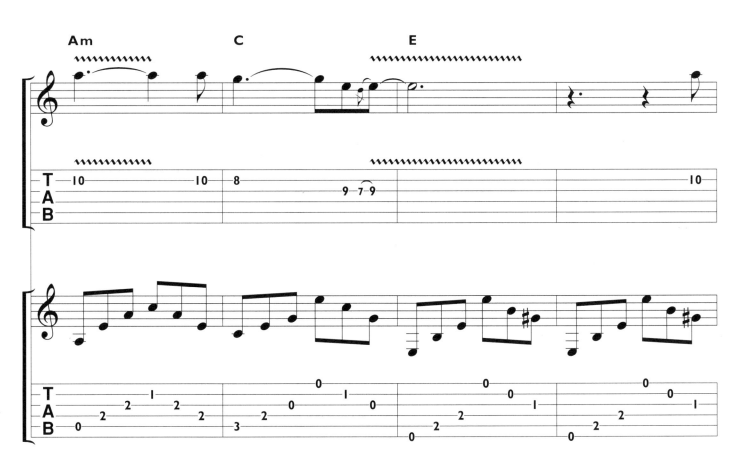

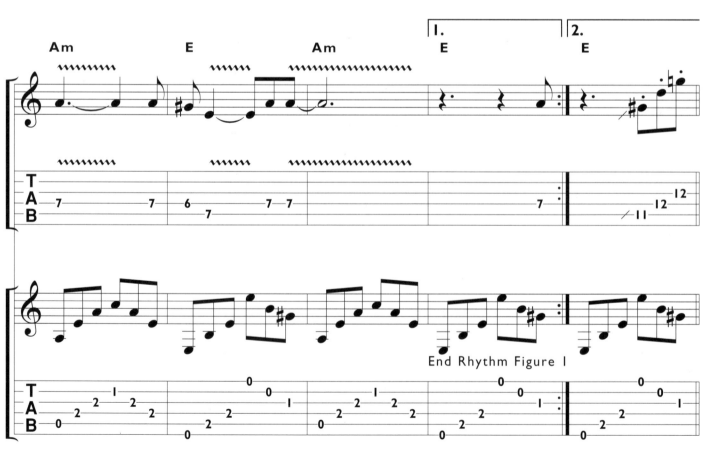

End Rhythm Figure I

Guitar I

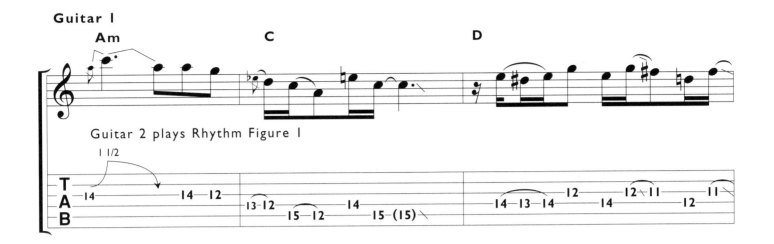

Guitar 2 plays Rhythm Figure 1

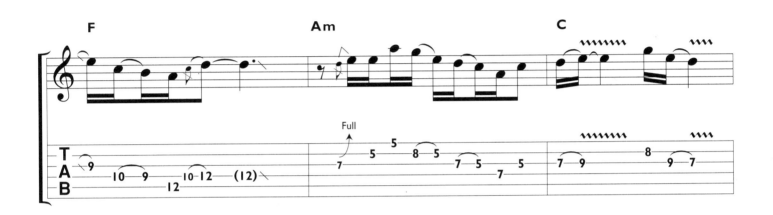

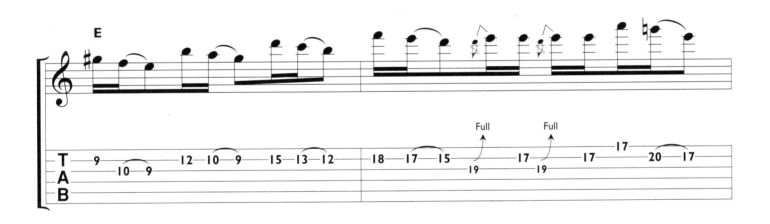

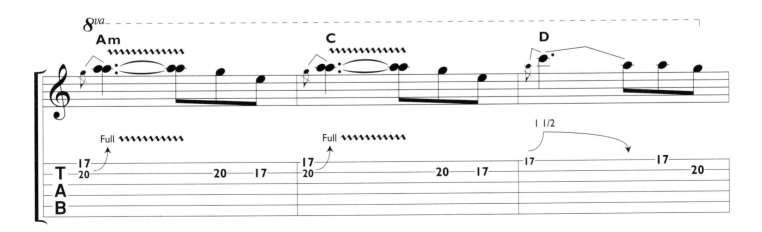

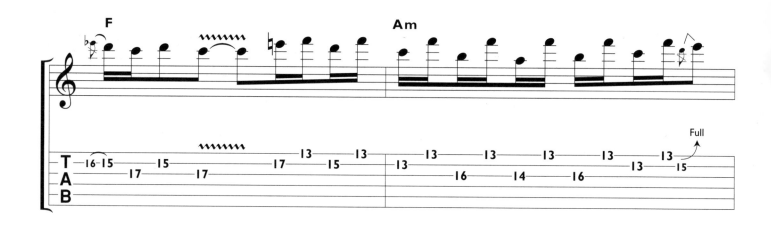

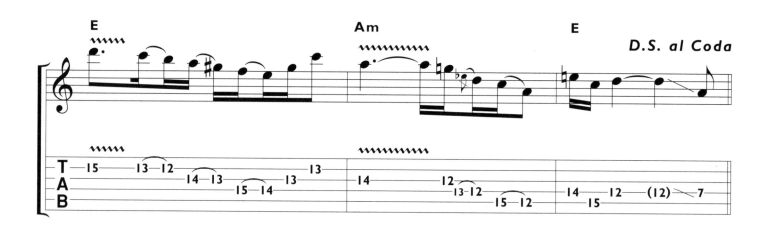

CD 2
TRACK 4

TRACK 5
Without
RHYTHM
GUITAR

TRACK 6
Without
LEAD
GUITAR

I AIN'T GOT NOBODY

Guitar 2

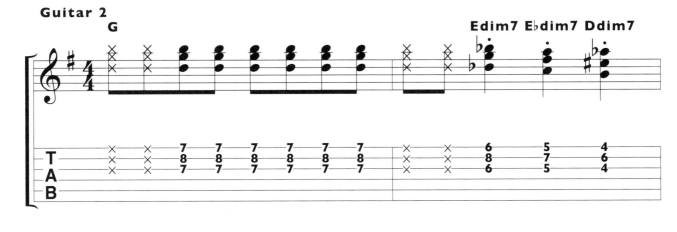

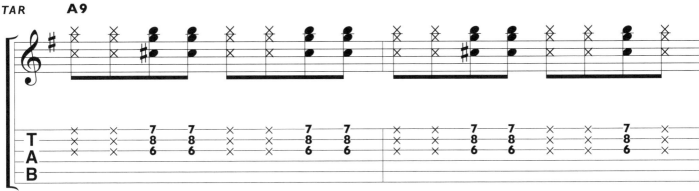

Guitar 1

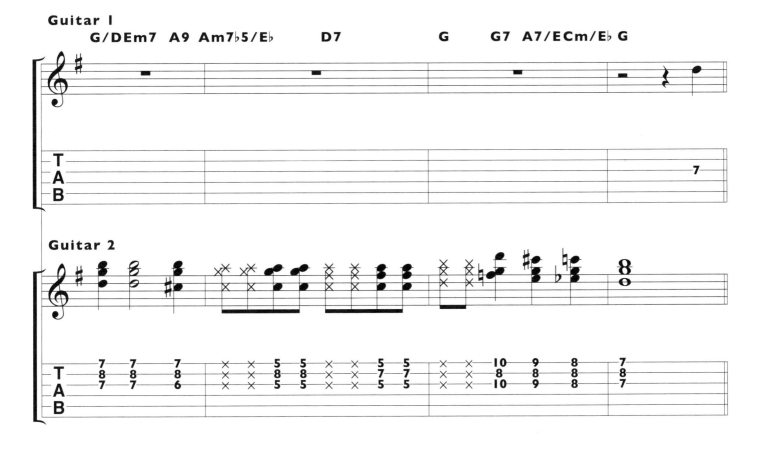

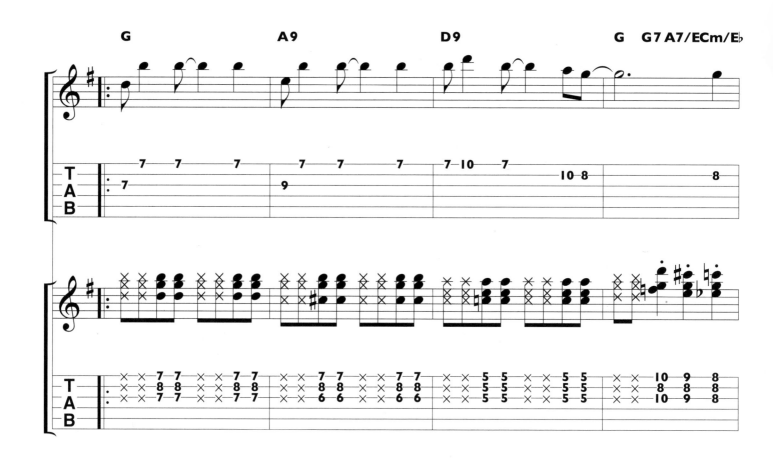

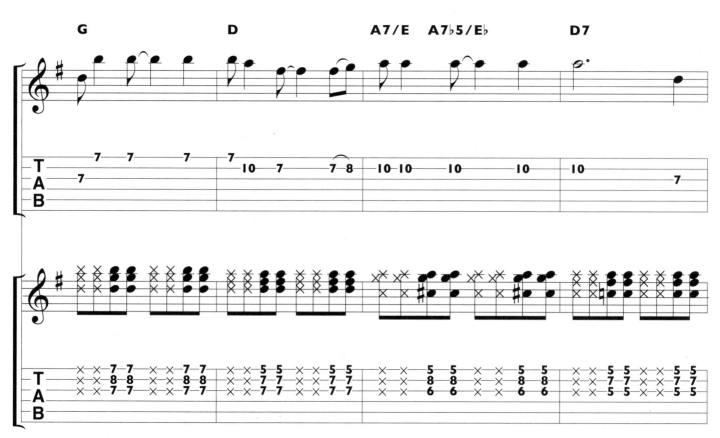

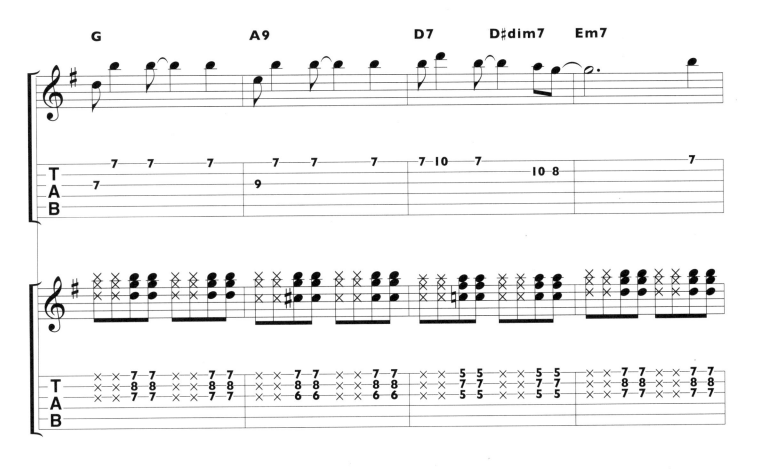

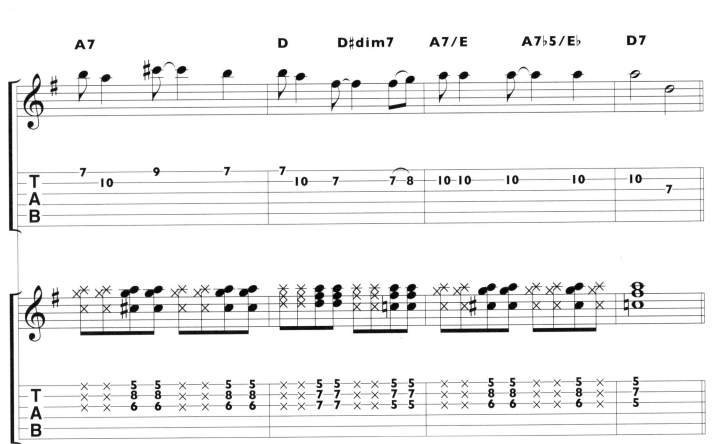

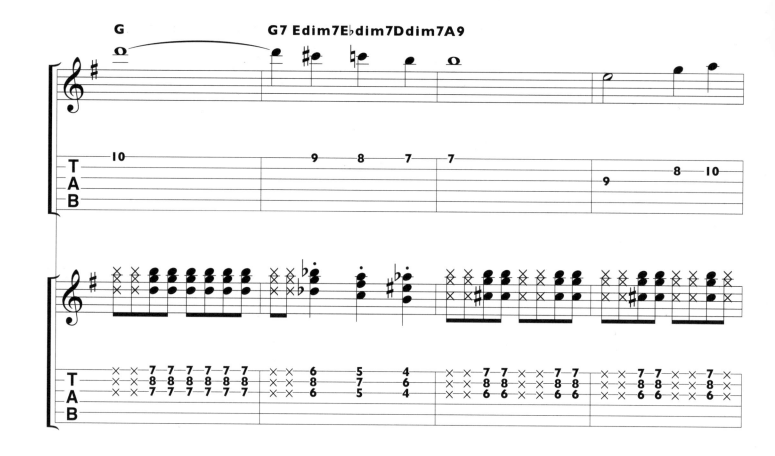

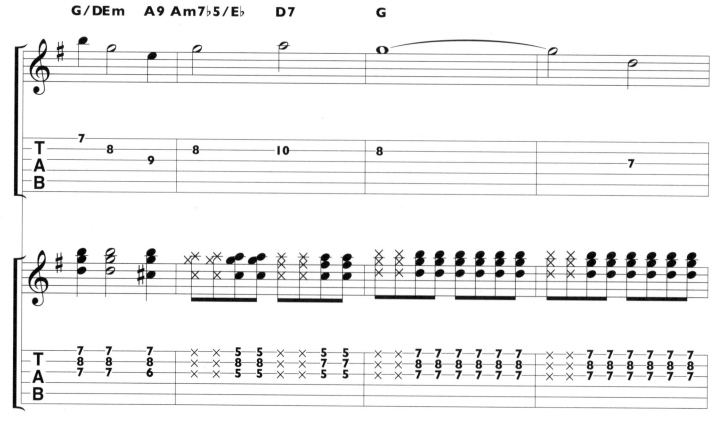

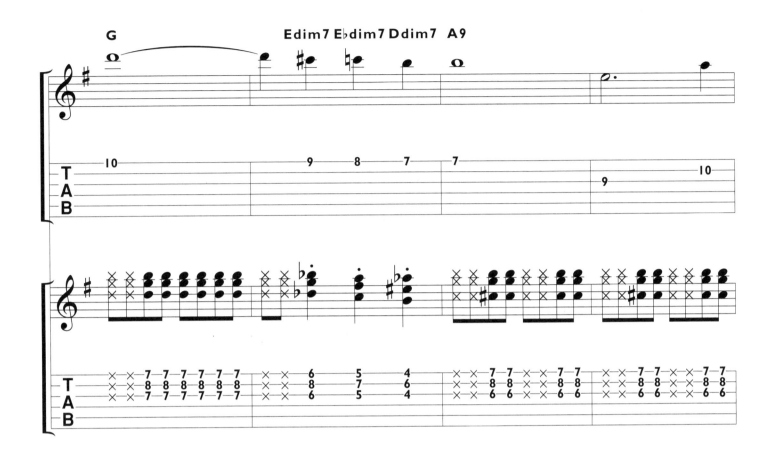

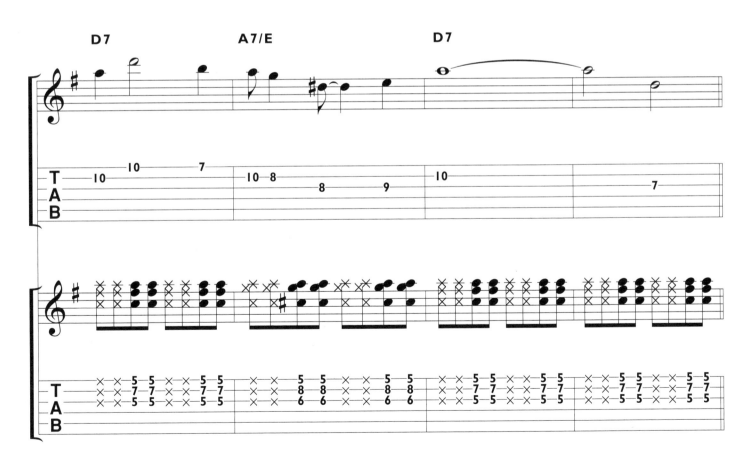

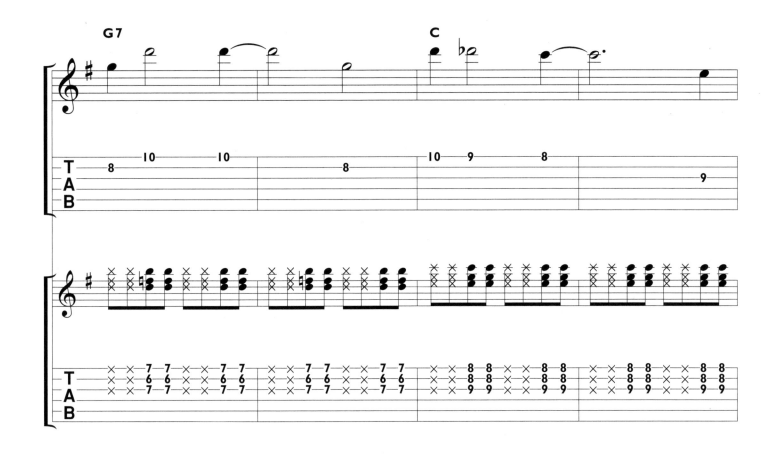

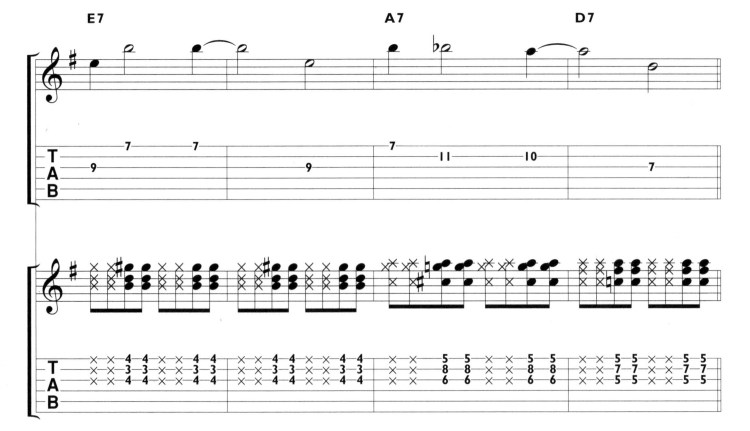

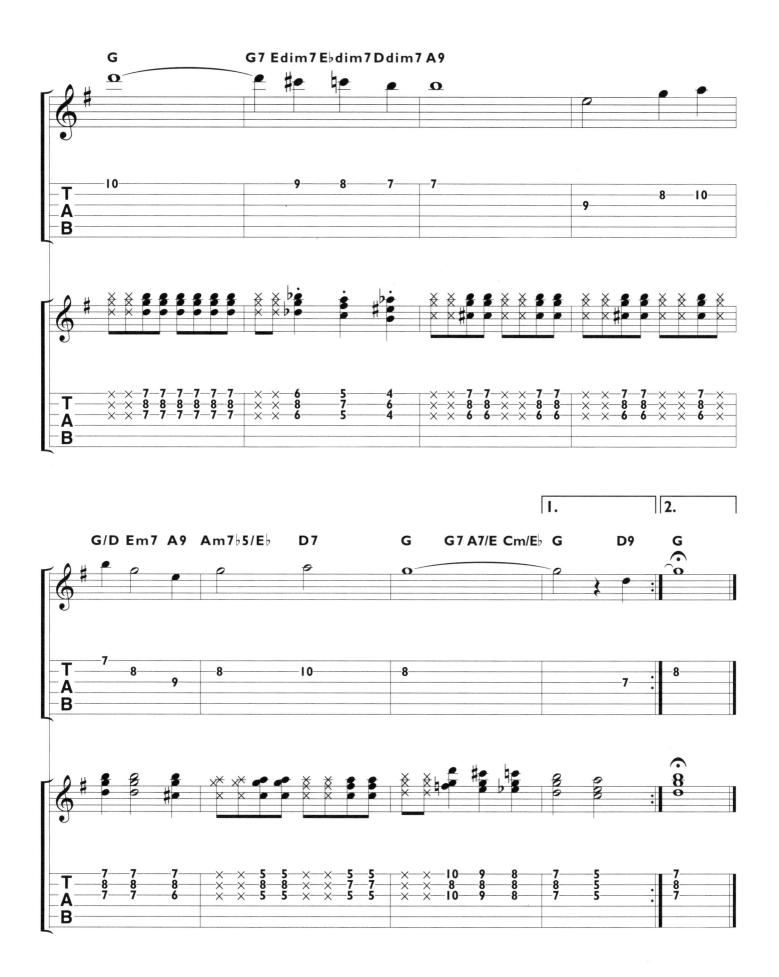

113

CD 2
TRACK 7

TRACK 8
Without
**RHYTHM
GUITAR**

TRACK 9
Without
**LEAD
GUITAR**

C C RIDER

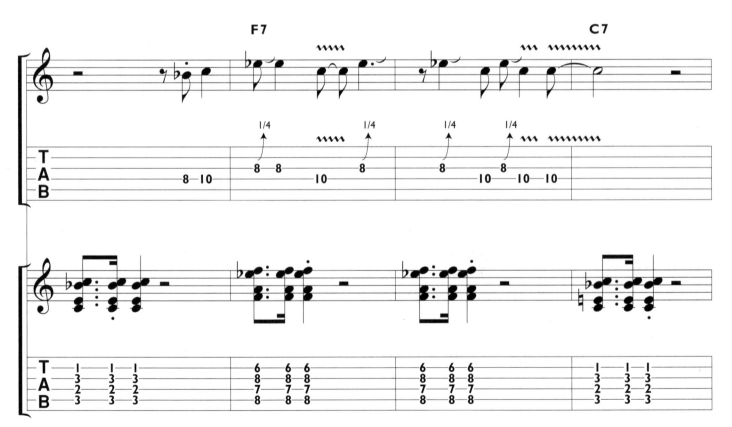

Guitar 1

Guitar 2 plays Rhythm Figure 1

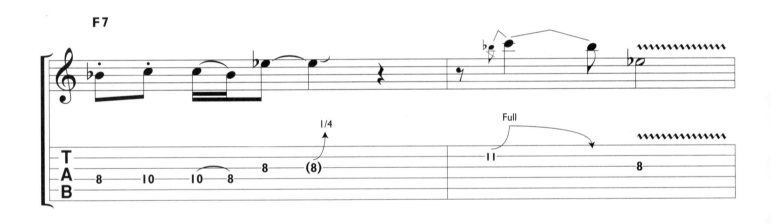

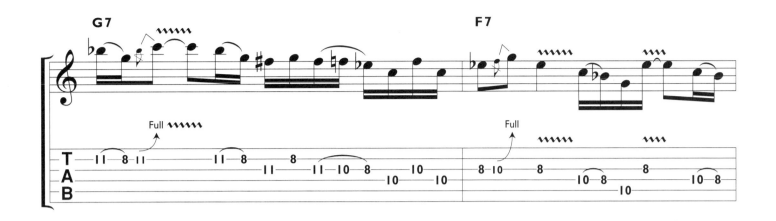

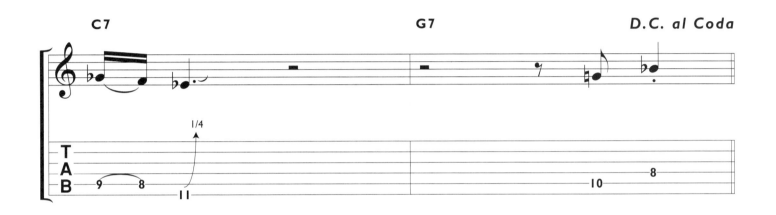

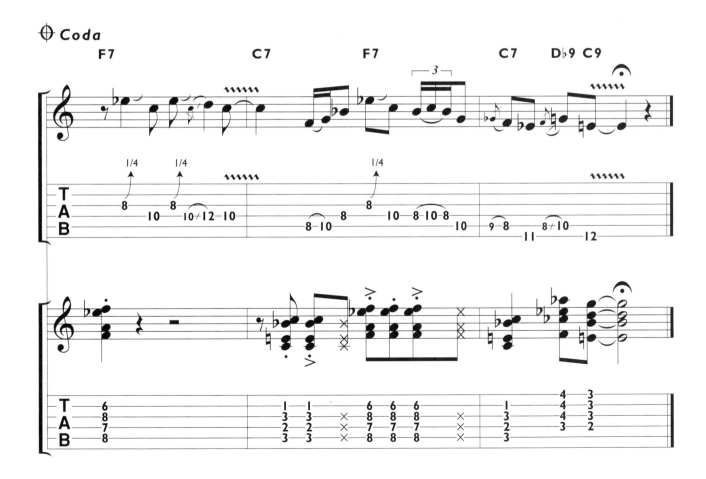

THIS TRAIN

CD 2
TRACK 10

TRACK 11
Without
RHYTHM
GUITAR

TRACK 12
Without
LEAD
GUITAR

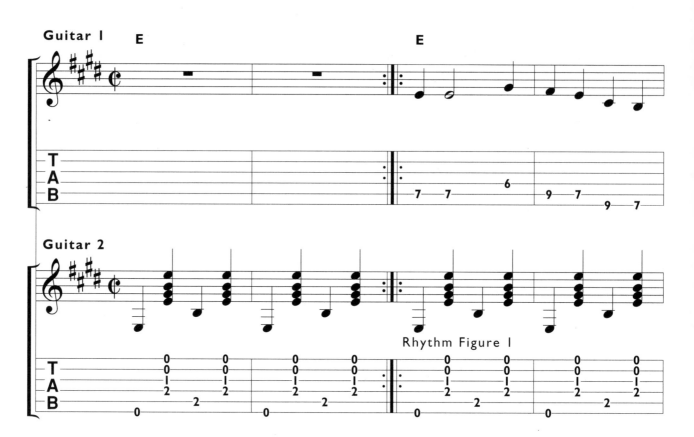

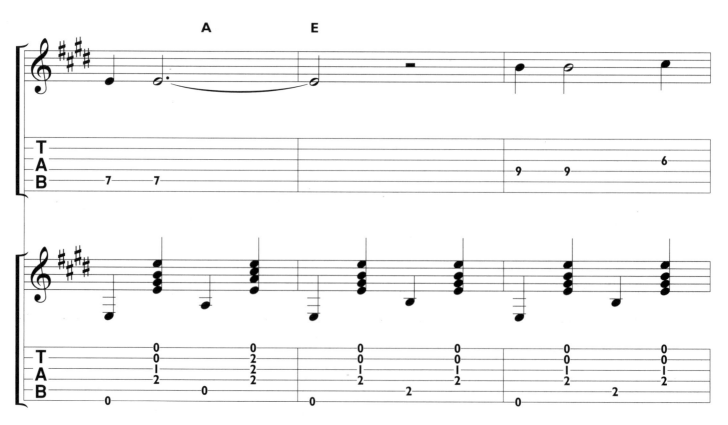

118

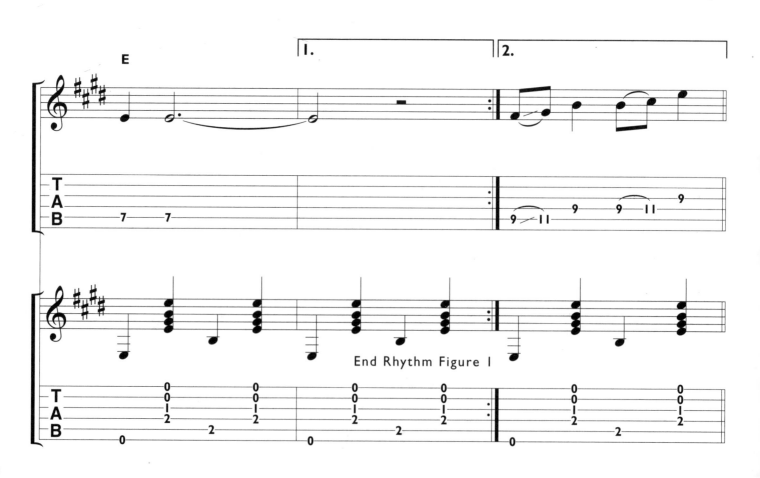

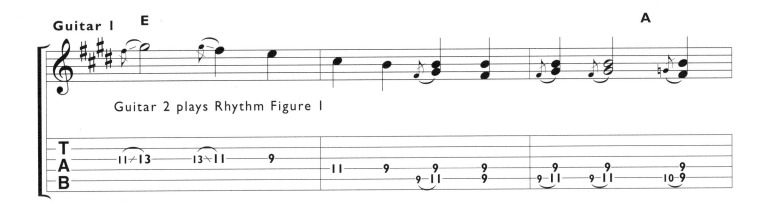

Guitar 2 plays Rhythm Figure I

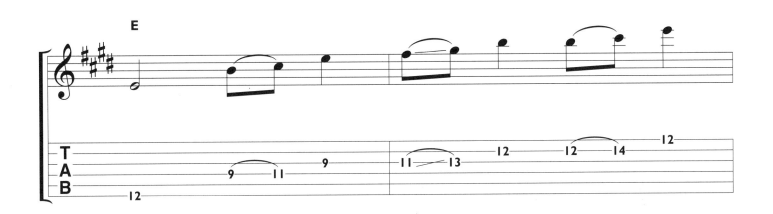

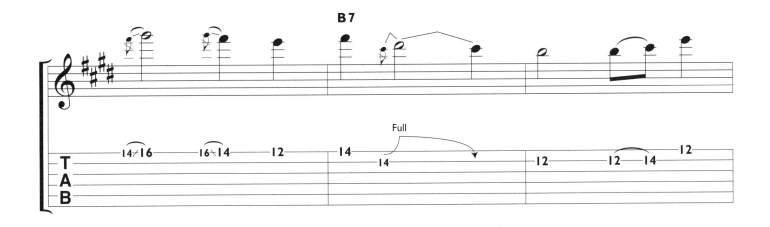

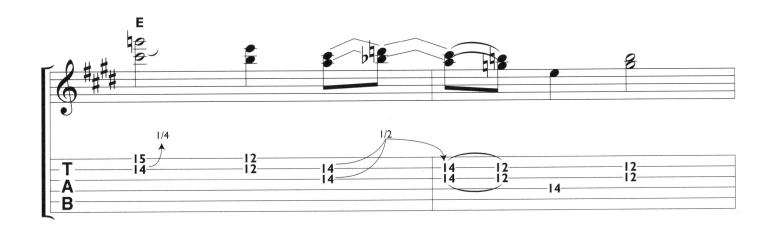

121

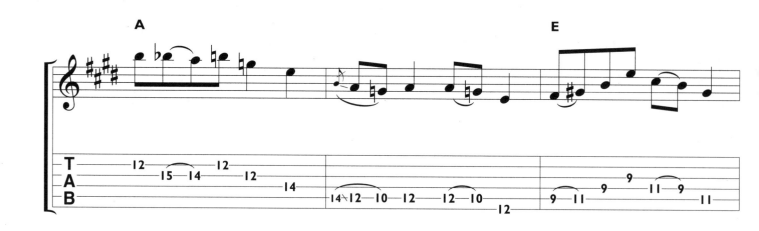

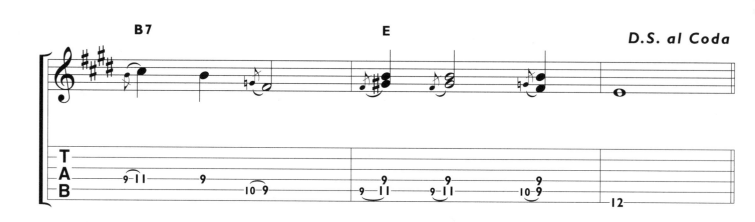

D.S. al Coda

⊕ *Coda*

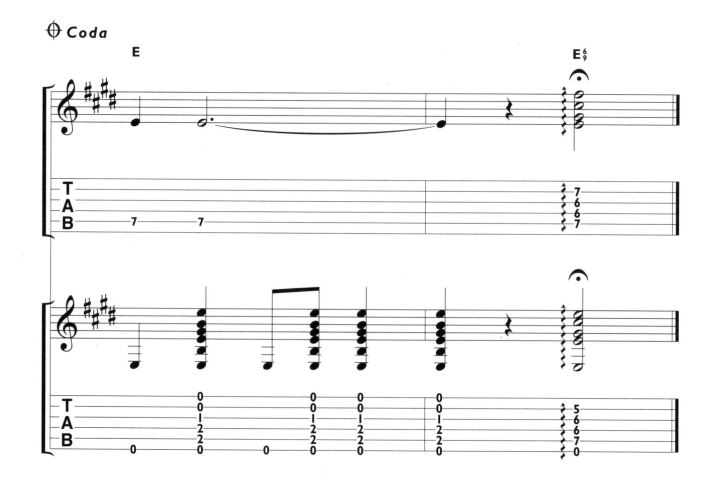

ST JAMES INFIRMARY

CD 2
TRACK 13

TRACK 14
Without
**RHYTHM
GUITAR**

TRACK 15
Without
**LEAD
GUITAR**

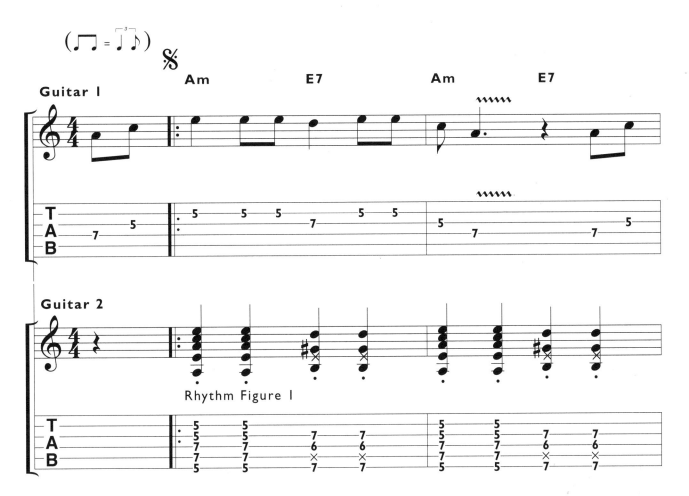
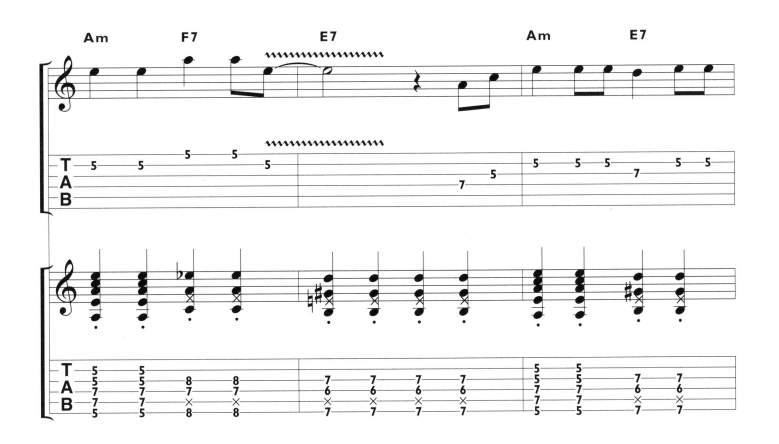

Rhythm Figure 1

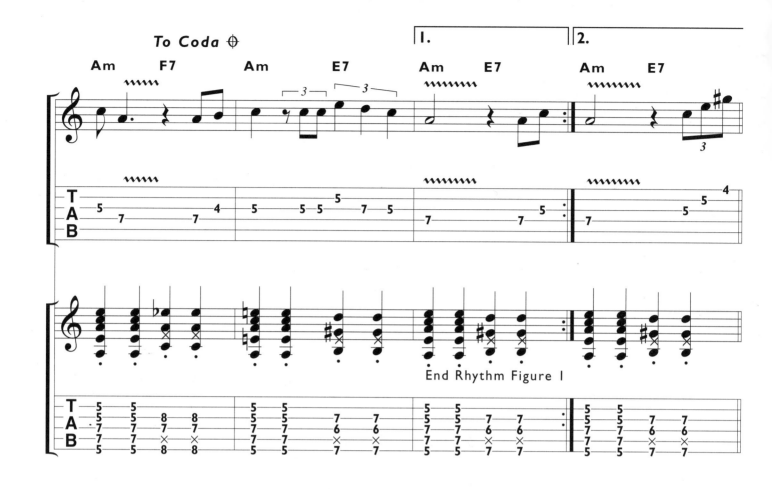

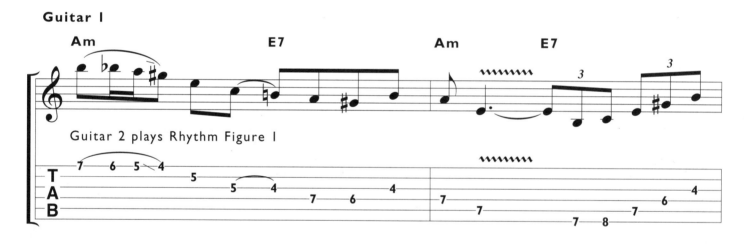

Guitar 1

Guitar 2 plays Rhythm Figure 1

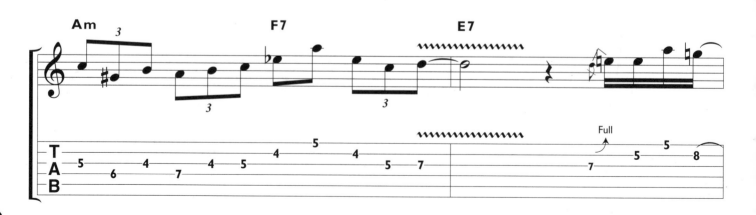

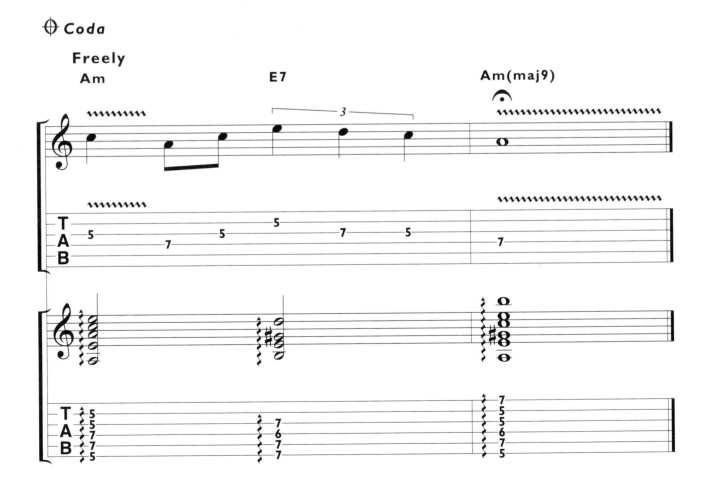

GUITAR TABLATURE EXPLAINED

Guitar music can be notated in three different ways: on a musical stave, in tablature, and in rhythm slashes.

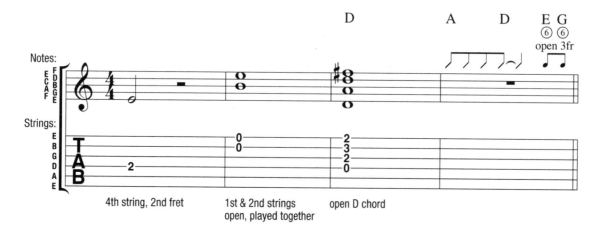

RHYTHM SLASHES

Are written above the stave. Strum chords in the rhythm indicated. Round noteheads indicate single notes.

THE MUSICAL STAVE

Shows pitches and rhythms and is divided by lines into bars. Pitches are named after the first seven letters of the alphabet.

TABLATURE

Graphically represents the guitar fingerboard. Each horizontal line represents a string, and each number represents a fret.

DEFINITIONS FOR SPECIAL GUITAR NOTATION

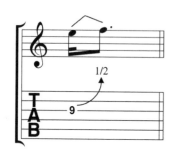

SEMI-TONE BEND

Strike the note and bend up a semi-tone (1/2 step).

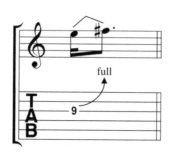

WHOLE-TONE BEND

Strike the note and bend up a whole-tone (whole step).

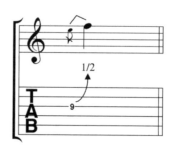

GRACE NOTE BEND

Strike the note and bend as indicated. Play the first note as quickly as possible.

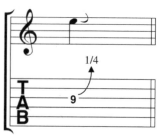

QUARTER-TONE BEND

Strike the note and bend up a 1/4 step.

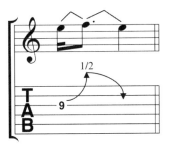

BEND & RELEASE
Strike the note and bend up as indicated, then release back to the original note.

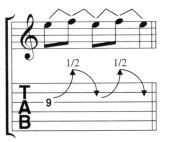

COMPOUND BEND & RELEASE
Strike the note and bend up and down in the rhythm indicated.

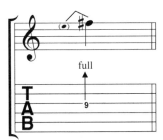

PRE-BEND
Bend the note as indicated, then strike it.

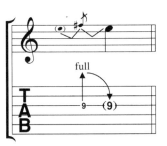

PRE-BEND & RELEASE
Bend the note as indicated. Strike it and release the note back to the original pitch.

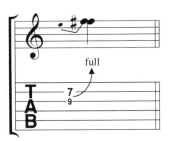

UNISON BEND
Strike the two notes simultaneously and bend the lower note up to the pitch of the higher.

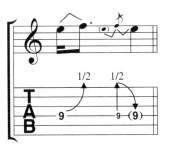

BEND & RESTRIKE
Strike the note and bend as indicated then restrike the string where the symbol occurs.

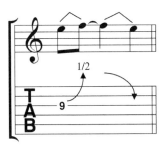

BEND, HOLD & RELEASE
Same as Bend & Release but hold the bend for the duration of the tie.

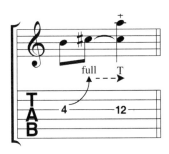

·BEND & TAP
Bend the note as indicated and tap the higher fret while still holding the bend.

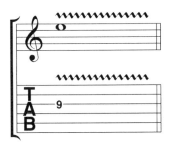

VIBRATO
The string is vibrated by rapidly bending and releasing the note with the fretting hand.

HAMMER-ON
Strike the first note with one finger, then sound the second note (on the same string) with another finger by fretting it without picking.

PULL-OFF
Place both fingers on the notes to be sounded, strike the first note and without picking, pull the finger off to sound the second note.

LEGATO SLIDE (GLISS)
Strike the first note and then slide the same frethand finger up or down to the second note. The second note is not struck.

SHIFT SLIDE (GLISS & RESTRIKE)
Same as Legato Slide, except the second note is struck.

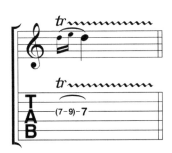

TRILL
Very rapidly alternate between the notes indicated by continuously hammering on and pulling off.

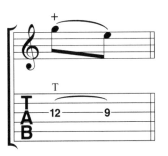

TAPPING
Hammer (tap) the fret indicated with the pick-hand index or middle finger and pull off to the note fretted by the fret hand.

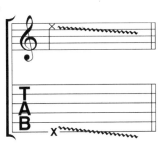

PICK SCRAPE
The edge of the pick is rubbed down (or up) the string, producing a scratchy sound.

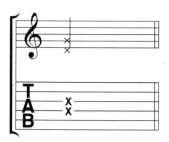

MUFFLED STRINGS

A percussive sound is produced by laying the fret hand across the string(s) without depressing, and striking them with the pick hand.

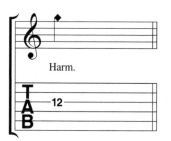

NATURAL HARMONIC

Strike the note while the fret-hand lightly touches the string directly over the fret indicated.

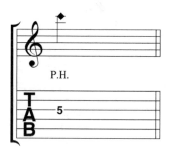

PINCH HARMONIC

The note is fretted normally and a harmonic is produced by adding the edge of the thumb or the tip of the index finger of the pick hand to the normal pick attack.

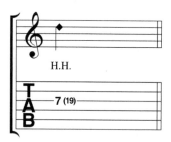

HARP HARMONIC

The note is fretted normally and a harmonic is produced by gently resting the pick hand's index finger directly above the indicated fret (in brackets) while plucking the appropriate string.

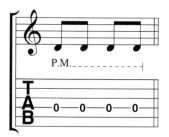

PALM MUTING

The note is partially muted by the pick hand lightly touching the string(s) just before the bridge.

RAKE

Drag the pick across the strings indicated with a single motion.

TREMOLO PICKING

The note is picked as rapidly and continuously as possible.

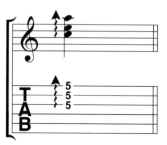

ARPEGGIATE

Play the notes of the chord indicated by quickly rolling them from top to bottom.

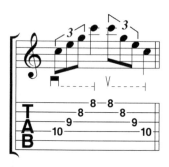

SWEEP PICKING

Rhythmic downstroke and/or upstroke motion across the strings.

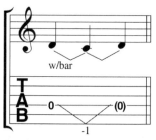

VIBRATO DIVE BAR & RETURN

The pitch of the note or chord is dropped a specific number of steps (in rhythm) then returned to the original pitch.

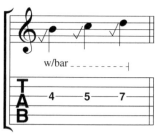

VIBRATO BAR SCOOP

Depress the bar just before striking the note, then quickly release the bar.

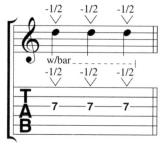

VIBRATO BAR DIP

Strike the note and then immediately drop a specific number of steps, then release back to the original pitch.

ADDITIONAL MUSICAL DEFINITIONS

ACCENT

Accentuate note (play louder).

ACCENT

Accentuate note with great intensity.

STACCATO

Shorten time value of note.

Downstroke.

Upstroke.

NOTE

Tablature numbers in brackets mean:

1. The note is sustained, but a new articulation (such as hammer-on or slide) begins.

2. A note may be fretted but not necessarily played.

D.%. al Coda

Go back to the sign %, then play until the bar marked *To Coda* ⊕ then skip to the section ⊕ *Coda*.

D.C. al Fine

Go back to the beginning and play until the bar marked *Fine*.

tacet

Instrument is silent (drops out).

Repeat bars between repeat signs.

When a repeated section has different endings, play the first ending only the first time and the second ending only the second time.